An Unauthorized Guide to

Pillsbury® Doughboy™ Collectibles

Jane Ann Boyd

Schiffer Publishing Ltd

4880 Lower Valley Road, Atglen, PA 19310 USA

Acknowledgments

Special thanks is given to my husband, Burt Hickcox. Without his support and help, this book would never have been possible. He has been a tremendous help in getting the pictures, making phone calls on my behalf, and completing details while I worked a full-time job.

I also thank George Fischler for his suggestions and time spent teaching us how to take photographs for this book.

Without the enthusiasm of my family and friends, this book could not have been written. My warmest thanks go to all who lent their support and gave me encouragement. Special thanks go to those who read the book before publication and gave me suggestions for improvements, especially Mary Smith.

I particularly thank my line dance class, who stuck with me even though my mind was not always on line dancing.

And finally, I thank Peter Schiffer for considering and publishing this book.

Library of Congress Catalog Control Number: 2004100763

Designed by Mark David Bowyer
Type set in DomBold BT / Aldine721 BT

ISBN: 0-7643-2076-9
Printed in China
1 2 3 4

Published by Schiffer Publishing Ltd.
4880 Lower Valley Road
Atglen, PA 19310
Phone: (610) 593-1777; Fax: (610) 593-2002
E-mail: info@schifferbooks.com
For the largest selection of fine reference books on this and related subjects, please visit our web site at
www.schifferbooks.com
We are always looking for people to write books on new and related subjects. If you have an idea for a book, please contact us at the above address.

This book may be purchased from the publisher.
Include $3.95 for shipping. Please try your bookstore first.
You may write for a free catalog.

In Europe, Schiffer books are distributed by
Bushwood Books
6 Marksbury Ave. Kew Gardens
Surrey TW9 4JF England
Phone: 44 (0)20 8392-8585; Fax: 44 (0)20 8392-9876
E-mail: info@bushwoodbooks.co.uk
Free postage in the UK. Europe: air mail at cost.
Please try your bookstore first.

Contents

Introduction

Welcome to Pillsbury Doughboy™ Collectibles

The world of Pillsbury Doughboy™ collectibles is exciting. Since his creation in 1965, the Pillsbury Doughboy's™ popularity has grown with collectors and dealers alike.

This book is a reference guide to help you with pricing or purchasing Doughboy™ collectibles. Pieces shown here are distributed in the United States with the approval of The Pillsbury Company®, however Doughboy™ items made in countries outside the United States may not have authorization from The Pillsbury Company®. There are also many handcrafted items being introduced to the market. Handcrafted indicates an individual produces an item, using pre-existing magnets, stickers, or etchings of the Doughboy™. If you purchase an item on a web site, be sure to ask the seller if it is handcrafted when you are not sure of the item's origin. This book does not cover handcraft pieces, since they are not authorized by Pillsbury®.

Throughout this book you will see the names The Pillsbury Company®, Pillsbury Doughboy™, and character names. Pillsbury® and the Doughboy™ character are registered trademarks of Pillsbury Company®, Minneapolis, MN 55402. All rights reserved.

A Little Company History

Pillsbury, a trusted name in baking products, was founded in 1869 when Charles Pillsbury purchased the Minneapolis Flour Mills, launching his career in the milling business. Charles Pillsbury could not have envisioned the growth and acquisition the company would eventually achieve. Pillsbury flour and baking products have always stood for high quality. In order to bring awareness to the company's standards for high quality, the Pillsbury® Best trademark with four X's was introduced on sacks of flour in 1872.

When Pillsbury® celebrated its 80th anniversary in 1949, the company wanted a new way to promote their products and generate new recipes. They introduced The Pillsbury Bake-Off Contest® and entrants competed for a shared prize purse of $70,000 that was disbursed among the top finalists. Thousands of contestants flocked to the Waldorf Astoria Hotel in New York City, where the contest was held.

In 1950, Pillsbury® began acquiring other companies, the first of which was Ballard and Ballard. With this acquisition, Pillsbury® began producing fresh dough. In 1957, the first refrigerated cookie dough was introduced. Consumers liked the new product that made it easy to open a package of refrigerated cookie dough and produce hot cookies with no mixing or clean up. To advertise the fresh dough and refrigerated dough products, Pillsbury® introduced the Pillsbury Doughboy™. He first appeared as "Poppin Fresh"® on November 7, 1965, in his commercial television debut popping out of a can of crescent rolls.

The Doughboy™ rose to stardom quickly. Viewers quickly came to recognize him by his giggle–"Hoo Hoo!" As noted on the Doughboy's 30th Birthday Collector's glass, his belly had been poked 32,500 times. That's a lot of giggles.

"Poppin Fresh" has starred in numerous commercials which have not changed much over the years. In early commercials, he was shown in a kitchen assisting with the baking. "Poppin" could be found passing biscuits or helping to decorate cookies. Since then, he has become versatile. You might have seen him as an opera singer, a rap artist, or a painter and he seemed to enjoy skateboarding across counter tops. You may even remember him playing musical instruments.

Today, the Doughboy™ is America's most popular food product character. Through the grapevine it was said that he lost popularity one year when the California Raisins appeared, but the following year Doughboy™ popped back to the top of the popularity charts.

In the early 1970s, Pillsbury introduced Poppin's wife, Poppie®, in a commercial. The rest of the Doughboy family soon followed. Bun Bun® is their daughter and Popper® is their son. Grandpopper® and Grandmommer® are the grandparents and they have a pet dog, Flapjack®, and a cat, Biscuit®.

Numerous toys today now include vinyl, cloth, and porcelain dolls, finger puppets, and many others. Finger puppets of Poppin, Poppie, Bun Bun, Popper, Flapjack, and Biscuit were introduced in 1974. They even had a house to live in.

To promote the Doughboy, as well as Pillsbury® products, Pillsbury offered items to give away, including vinyl and beanie dolls. Special boxes of Grands Biscuits also contained a Doughboy™ beanie doll as well as the two cans of biscuits.

The Doughboy™ now appears on almost all of the Pillsbury® products and even products that use Pillsbury® components. While walking through your grocery store, you can play a game with your children to see who can spot the first or the most pictures of the Doughboy™. This will keep your children occupied and it is fun to see where he shows up. He can be found in the cake aisle, frozen food section, and several other areas of the store. See where the Doughboy™ pops up.

The acquisition of many companies over the years has helped Pillsbury® to introduce many new consumer products and expand its standards of high quality. In 1967, Pillsbury® entered the fast food market with the acquisition of Burger King. In 1975, the company acquired Totino's Finer Foods and entered the pizza business. It acquired canned vegetable products when the Jolly Green Giant became part of the Pillsbury® family in 1979. When Pillsbury® purchased Haagen-Dazs ice cream in 1983, it entered another field of almost universal enjoyment.

Pillsbury® was bought by the United Kingdom-based company Grand Metropolitan plc. in 1989. Grandmet later merged with Guinness to form Diageo. The Pillsbury® name and the Doughboy™ were retained throughout all these changes. One of the world's largest food companies was created in 2001, when General Mills® acquired Pillsbury®.

About the Collectibles Collection

Over 250 Doughboy™ items are listed in this book, with dates ranging from 1971 to 2003. Only items associated with the Pillsbury Doughboy™ line are included. Each item is described with the year of manufacture, the approximate height and width, and the company of manufacture. A picture is provided of each item.

The Doughboy™ has become very popular since its inception, and a substantial number of items have been produced by numerous companies. Most of these products are marked with the year of manufacture and the manufacturing company's name, however this may not always be the case. Some producers and distributors include The Pillsbury Company®, Benjamin & Medwin, Inc., Anchor Hocking, Correll, Danbury Mint, and Barth & Dreyfuss of California. The largest producers and/or distributors appear to be The Pillsbury Company® and Benjamin & Medwin. Some items are marked T.P.C. This refers to The Pillsbury Company®.

An item not found in a box should be inspected thoroughly. Items purchased from a website should have a clear description, and you should ask questions of the seller if you are not familiar with the product. Many items sold on the WEB may be handcrafted, that is made by an individual and not authorized by Pillsbury®.

Pricing the Collectibles

This book is designed to provide you with a reference guide to help with pricing and purchasing Doughboy™ collectibles that are on the market today. Keep in mind that the information is just a guide.

Prices are determined by demand, quantity, and condition. The condition of the item is one of the most important factors in determining its value. The prices given in this book are for items in mint condition. Mint condition means that they should be unused, such as those just taken out of the original box or packaging. Items that show wear, scratches, chips, stains, and cracks would have lower prices. How much value the item losses depends upon the condition of the item, where you live, and how much you are willing to pay for or sell the item for.

The values of items in this book are estimated values and retail values. Estimated values have been determined by researching items sold on the internet, in antique shops and flea markets, and at auctions. Retail values are prices of items that are still being sold on the market today.

Chapter 1

Dolls & Figurines

Find your favorite doll or figurine in this chapter. Dolls are made of plastic, vinyl, cloth, and rubber. You will be able to find the Doughboy family finger puppets, the Grandpopper, and the Grandmommer. Figurines of the Doughboy can be found made of resin and porcelain. The Doughboy calendar, Collector Figurines, and the International Figurines are all displayed and many more.

Poppie Fresh® Vinyl Doll. Poppie is wearing her bonnet and dress with a blue pocket. Poppie comes with a stand that has her name, "Poppie Fresh", on it. Date can be found on back of Poppie's collar. 1972 The Pillsbury Company. 6" in height including the stand, stand is 4" x 2 1/2", $25 to $35

Poppin Fresh® Vinyl Doll. The Doughboy™ is wearing his trademark chef's hat and scarf. The Doughboy™ comes with a stand that has his name, "Poppin Fresh", on it. Date can be located on the back of the Doughboy's™ hat. 1971 The Pillsbury Company®. 7 1/2" in height including the stand, stand is 4" x 2 1/2", $25 to $35

Vinyl Doughboy™ Doll. Date can be located on the back of the Doughboy's™ hat. 1995 The Pillsbury Company®, made in China. 7" in height, $10 to $15

Vinyl Doughboy™ Doll. The Pillsbury® name is engraved in a light blue circle on the Doughboy's™ hat. Date can be located on the back of the Doughboy's™ hat. 1971 The Pillsbury Company®, Minneapolis, Minn. 7" in height, $20 to $25

Vinyl Doughboy™ Doll. On the chef's hat in the dark blue circle the Pillsbury® name is printed in white. Date located on the back of the hat. 1971 T.P.C. (The Pillsbury Company®). 7" in height, $10 to $15

Mini Doughboy™ Beanie Dolls. The beanie doll was available in packages and boxes of Grands Biscuits. The dolls in Grands Biscuits were not packaged in a bag. The blue tag attached to the Doughboy's™ hand is his birth certificate. Date located on the sewn on label: 1999 The Pillsbury Company®, Hand made in China. 5 1/2" in height, $8 to $10

Pillsbury Giggling Doughboy™ with Bake Off Apron. This Doughboy™ is plush and giggles when you squeeze his stomach. He comes with a bake off apron. Date produced located on label. 1999 The Pillsbury Company®, Creation by Dakin.16" in height, $16 to $20

Doughboy™ in a Can. The Doughboy™ looks like he is popping right out of the can when you open it. The Doughboy™ is made of a soft rubber material and comes with a built in stand. Date is found on the can. 1997 The Pillsbury Company®, Creative Imaginations. 6" Rubber Doughboy™, Can is 8 1/4" in height 3" in diameter, $15 to $20

Resin Doughboy™ Figurines. There are four Doughboys™ in this set, each are sold separately. Each Doughboy™ is illustrated in this book. The set include the Doughboy™ Holding a Cookie, Doughboy™ Holding a Rollin Pin, Doughboy™ Holding a Pan of Biscuits and the Doughboy™ Holding Hands Out. This set can be recognized easily. It has Pillsbury written across the blue base that each Doughboy™ stands on. The following information can be located on the base: 1997 The Pillsbury Company®, Distributed by: Creative Imagination Inc., Made in China. Each Doughboy is 5" in height with a 2 1/2" diameter base, $20.00 to $30.00

Doughboy™ Holding a Cookie

Doughboy™ Holding a Rolling Pin

Doughboy™ Holding a Pan of Biscuits

Doughboy™ Holding Hands Out

Grandpopper Vinyl Doll. The Grandpopper looks very handsome with his mustache, dressed in a vest with three blue buttons and bow tie. The date is located on the back of the vest. 1974 The Pillsbury Company®. 5" in height, $55 to $65

Grandmommer Vinyl Doll. Grandmommer is wearing a dress with a ruffled collar and a blue pocket. Her hair is done up in a bun and she wears glasses. Date can be found on the back of the dress under the collar. 1974 The Pillsbury Company®, 4 3/4" in height, $55 to $65

Poppie Finger Puppet. Poppie is dressed in an apron with a blue pocket which ties in the back in a bow. She has a bonnet on her head which is tied around her neck. Poppie's name and date can be found around the base. 1974 The Pillsbury Company®. 3 1/2" in height, $40 to $45

Doughboy™ "Poppin Fresh" Finger Puppet. Poppin is dressed in his usual attire: chef's hat and kerchief. Poppin Fresh name and date can be found on the base of this finger puppet. 1974 The Pillsbury Company®, 4 1/4" in height, $40 to $45

Popper Finger Puppet. Popper is wearing a blue billed baseball cap and kerchief, which is tied in the back. Popper's name and date can be found on the base. 1974 The Pillsbury Company®. 3 1/4" in height, $40 to $45

Bun Bun Finger Puppet. Bun Bun has a blue heart on the front of her bib. A bow is in her hair. Bun Bun's name and date is found on the base. 1974 The Pillsbury Company®. 3 1/8" in height, $40 to $45

Biscuit Finger Puppet. Biscuit is wearing a scarf with a blue bow, has pointed ears, blue eyes. Biscuit has one paw in the air. Biscuit's name and date are on the base. 1974 The Pillsbury Company®. 3" in height, $45 to $50

Flapjack Finger Puppet. Flapjack has floppy ears, a short tail and wears a collar. Flapjack's name and date is found on the base. 1974 The Pillsbury Company®. 2 1/4" in height, $45 to $50

Poppie Fresh & Her Pals, Bun Bun and Biscuit. See individual pieces for more details. Poppie and her pals are in their original box. Seal has never been broken. 1974 The Pillsbury Company®. Box is 7 1/2" by 5 3/4", Poppie is 3 1/2" in height, Bun Bun is 3 1/8" in height, and Biscuit is 3" in height, $135 to $155

Poppie Cloth Doll. Poppie is made of a cloth material, wearing a cotton bonnet and apron. The apron has lace around the bottom and a blue embroidered flower on the side. Date can be located on tag. 1972 The Pillsbury Company®, Made in Taiwan. 8" in height, $15 to $20

Giggling Doughboy™ Beanbag. The Doughboy™ is made of a plush soft cotton type material. He is accented with his chief's hat and scarf. When you press his stomach he giggles. Body is filled with plastic pellets. Item is marked on label: 1999 The Pillsbury Company®, Applause Inc., Made in China. 9" in height, $12 to $20

Pillsbury Doughboy Calendar

The Doughboy™ Calendar comes with twelve Doughboy™ figurines, each capturing the festivities of the month he is representing. The calendar is shown with all the pieces when complete. Calendar and Doughboy™ figures are sold separately. Each is pictured with details of the piece. The Doughboy Calendar comes with a numbered Certificate of Authenticity. Date can be found on Certificate and on each Doughboy™ piece. 1997 Danbury Mint.

Calendar is 15 3/4" wide by 22 1/2" in height, $20 to $25, Doughboy Figures range in size from 1 3/4" to 3 1/2" in height, $20 to $25, Total Cost $260 to $320

January. The Doughboy™ is ready to start the new year with his noise maker and delicious bundt cake. 3 1/8" in height, $20 to $25

March. Saint Patrick's Day has always been known for wearing of the green. The Doughboy™ is making no exceptions wearing his green vest with yellow shamrocks for decoration. 3" in height, $20 to $25

February. The Doughboy™ is decorating a pink heart cookie. 3" in height, $20 to $25

April. The Doughboy™ has his picnic basket full of goodies and his blue umbrella in case he encounters any April showers. 3 1/4" in height, $20 to $25

May. The Doughboy is taking time to relax. Sitting on his red checkered blanket with a matching napkin he enjoys his brownie treats. 2 1/2" in height, $20 to $25

June. The Doughboy is wearing his lavender striped apron and carrying a plate of hot dogs. 3” in height, $20 to $25

July. The Doughboy is decorating his cupcakes with red, white and blue sprinkles. The American flag tops the cupcake. 3 1/4" in height, $20 to $25

September. The Doughboy is reading his book, "ABC of Cooking", while eating a cookie. 2 1/2" in height, $20 to $25

August, The Doughboy enjoys lounging on a crescent with his sunglasses and sipping lemonade. 1 3/4" in height, $20 to $25

October. The Doughboy has his pumpkin carved and ready for the occasion. 2 3/4" in height, $20 to $25

December. The Doughboy is boxing up his favorite cookies to give as gifts. 3 1/2" in height, $20 to $25

November. The Doughboy has baked up a large pumpkin pie in a colorful pie pan. 3" in height, $20 to $25

Collector Dolls

Porcelain Collector Doll: Baked to Perfection. The Doughboy is carrying a plate of cookies, wearing his red checkered apron and blue mitt. Doll comes with a numbered Certificate of Authenticity. Date of item can be located on the Certificate or care Instruction tag. 1999 The Pillsbury Company, Danbury Mint. 12" in height, $69 to $78

Porcelain Collector Doll: Recipe Time. The Doughboy is relaxing on his braided rug while reading his favorite recipe book. You may arrange the Doughboy and book on the rug. This doll comes with a numbered Certificate of Authenticity. Date of item can be located on Certificate or care instruction tag, 2000 The Pillsbury Company, Danbury Mint. 8 1/2" in height, $69 to $78

Porcelain Collector Doll: Picnic Surprise. The Doughboy is kneeling on a rug arranging the item in a basket. He has a green backpack that he is wearing. In the basket there are bread sticks, cinnamon rolls and biscuits. They are made individually, allowing for personal arrangement. The Doughboy comes with a numbered Certificate of Authenticity. The date can be located on the Certificate or care instruction tag. 1999 The Pillsbury Company, Danbury Mint. 10" in height, $69 to $78

Porcelain Collector Doll: At Your Service. The Doughboy is all dressed in his tux ready to serve a plate of freshly baked crescent rolls. This Porcelain Collector Doll comes with a numbered Certificate of Authenticity. Date of item can be located on Certificate or care instruction tag. 2001 The Pillsbury Company, Danbury Mint. 11" in height, $69 to $78

Porcelain Collector Doll: The Pillsbury Doughboy Santa Doll. The Doughboy is dressed in a red vest and black belt, he has prepared a plate of cookies. His bag of goodies is ready to go filled with baked products that you arrange. Each Porcelain Collector Doll comes with a numbered Certificate of Authenticity. The date of the doll can be found on the Certificate or on the care instruction tag. 2002 The Pillsbury Company, Danbury Mint. 12 1/2" in height, $96 to $106

Porcelain Collector Doll: The Pillsbury Doughboy™ Holiday Baker. The Doughboy™ is wearing a green and red plaid vest, while his chef's hat is decorated with candy canes and holly leaves. The Doughboy is holding a wreath made of different shaped sugar cookies and holding a red bow. Star sugar cookies sit on a bench next to the Doughboy. Holiday Baker comes with a numbered Certificate of Authenticity. 2003 The Pillsbury Company, Danbury Mint. Approximately 12 1/2" in height, $96 to 106

Cookie Companions, The Doughboy holds a recipe book for his friend, Jenny. Jenny is made of fine porcelain and is hand painted. Jenny's blonde hair is braided with blue polka-dot ribbons tied in bows. Jenny is wearing blue bib overalls, rolled up to form a cuff at the bottom of her legs. Under the overalls she wears a white blouse trimmed in red. The Doughboy and Jenny are wearing fabric chef's hats and red striped aprons. The Doughboy is holding a recipe book for Frosted Heart Cookies while Jenny rolls out the dough. Cookie Companions come with a numbered Certificate of Authenticity. 2002 The Pillsbury Company, Danbury Mint. Approximately 16" in height, $108 to $118

Little Baking Buddies. The Doughboy introduces Becky his baking buddy. Becky is made of fine porcelain and is hand painted. Becky's head turns and you position her on the checkered base. Becky wears a flowered dress, white apron and fabric chef's hat. As she reaches for a cookie it appears she is going to poke the Doughboy in the stomach. The Doughboy is wearing his trademark fabric chef's hat, scarf, a striped apron and a blue mitt. Baking Buddies comes with a numbered Certificate of Authenticity. 2001 The Pillsbury Company, Danbury Mint. Approximately 13 1/2" in height, $108 to $118

Pillsbury Doughboy Collector Figurines

These adorable Pillsbury Doughboy figurines are a delightful series. No one can make cleanup and baking more fun than the Doughboy. These figurines are specially crafted of porcelain and named after the fun things that the Doughboy can find to do in the kitchen. The name can be found on the bottom of each figure. There are 12 figurines in all. Not all are shown. Figurines come with a numbered Certificate of Authenticity, date of item can be found on the Certificate. 2002 The Pillsbury Company, Danbury Mint. Sizes range from 4 1/4" to 6 7/8" in height, $23.00 to $30.00

Spreading It On Thick. The Doughboy is spreading pink icing as he holds a spatula in his hands. 4 1/2" in height, $23 to $30

Flour Power. The delightful Doughboy is getting a bag of flour to make more treats. 4 1/4" in height, $23 to $30

Honey of A Recipe. Two delicate honey bees watch while the Doughboy gathers honey for his sweet treat. 4 1/4" in height, $23 to $30

Recipe For Success. With measuring spoon in hand, the Doughboy measures the ingredients for a new recipe. 4 3/4" in height, $23 to $30

The Gravy Boat. This piece is adorable. The Doughboy appears to be rowing as he sits in a gravy boat with spoons in his hands. 4 1/2" in height, $23 to $30

The Unbeatable Chef. The Doughboy is mixing up his favorite recipe. 4 3/4" in height, $23 to $30

Bottom Up. The Doughboy is using a ladle as an umbrella. 6 7/8" in height, $23 to $30

Clean Sweep. The Doughboy is sweeping with his red handled pastry brush. 5 1/4" in height, $23 to $30

Springing Into Action. The Doughboy is having fun in the kitchen springing around on a whisk. 6 1/2" in height, $23 to $30

Pillsbury Doughboy International Figurines

The Pillsbury Doughboy has been helping us cook for over 30 years. Now he has gone international. Each Doughboy has the flare and continuity of the country he is depicting. There are 12 different countries represented. On the bottom of each Doughboy figure is the Country he is representing. The International Figurines come with a number Certificate of Authenticity. 2002 The Pillsbury Company, Danbury Mint. $23.00 to 30.00

Italy. While in Italy the Pillsbury Doughboy uses his skills to capture the hearts of all by demonstrating how he makes a pizza. 4 3/4" tall, $23 to $30

The Big Cheese. The Doughboy is standing on a block of cheese as he slides down a grater. 5 1/2" in height, $23 to $30

Ireland. In Ireland the Pillsbury Doughboy has the luck of the leprechaun. 4 3/4" tall, $23 to $30

United States. The Doughboy has finished baking his apple pie and is decorating it with the United States flag. 5 1/2" tall, $23 to $30

Scotland. Dressed in kilts, the Pillsbury Doughboy plays the bagpipe. 5" tall, $23 to $30

France. The Eiffel Tower stands on a crescent roll behind the Doughboy. He has a gray towel over his arm and a green bottle of wine with two pink wine glasses on his tray. 4 1/2" tall, $23 to $30

England. Standing on guard with his spoon ready, the Doughboy stands in front of a guard house wearing a red coat. 5" tall, $23 to $30

Spain. The Doughboy in the tradition of Spain is dressed as a Matador. Wearing a blue and gold bolero and waving his red cape, the Doughboy is ready to take on the cookie bull that stands behind him. 4 3/4" tall, $23 to $30

Egypt. The Doughboy uses fudge and graham crackers to make a pyramid. 4 1/2" in height, $23 to $30

China. The Doughboy stands inside a spoon while holding a pair of chop sticks. 5" in height, $23 to $30

Mexico. The Doughboy has a bowl of chips behind him, has a sombrero hanging around his neck, and is wearing a colorful poncho. The Doughboy's guitar has hanging from it red and green chilies. 4 3/4" in height, $23 to $30

Russia. Two columns stand behind the Doughboy as he kicks up his heels in a maroon shirt, tied with a sash. 5" in height, $23 to $30

Germany. The Doughboy is wearing a green jacket, standing on top of three cookbooks, holding up a cuckoo clock. 5 3/4" in height, $23 to $30

Chapter 2

Cookie Jars

There are 9 cookie jars featured in this chapter. The differences in the Funfetti sets produced in 1992 and 2001 are described below. Some of the cookie jars have other items in their series that can be found throughout this book.

Doughboy Cookie Jar. This is one of the first cookie jars made. This item is unmarked. 1973 The Pillsbury Company, Made in Japan, 10 1/2" in height, $50 to $55

Doughboy Baker Cookie Jar. As are all items in the Baker Series this cookie jar shows the Doughboy holding a plate of cookies. Item is marked on bottom. 1997 The Pillsbury Company, Benjamin & Medwin NY, NY, Made in China, 12" in height, $45 to $50

Doughboy Cookie Jar. Item marked on bottom. 1998 The Pillsbury Company. 12" in height, $40 to $45

Doughboy Giggle Cookie Jar. Store your goodies in this container and you will know when someone is getting a cookie with this giggle cookie jar. When the head is removed the Doughboy giggles—"Hoo Hoo!". Item is marked on bottom. 1999 The Pillsbury Company, Benjamin & Medwin Inc. NY, NY, Made in China. 12" in height, $50 to $55

Doughboy Cookie Jar. The pieces for the 2002 series are smaller in size than items made in pervious years. This cookie jar is marked on the bottom. 2002 The Pillsbury Company, Benjamin & Medwin Inc. 5 1/2" wide x 9 3/4" tall, $20 to $25

Pillsbury Doughboy Cookie Jar & Cookie Platter. These two items are sold as a set. Whether you're serving cookies to friends or family, this set is sure to delight everyone. The 3-D Cookie jar pictures the Doughboy holding one of his favorite cookies. An assortment of cookies surrounds the platter with the Doughboy embossed in the center to lend a hand. A numbered Certificate of Authenticity comes with this set. The set is marked on the bottom. 2002 The Pillsbury Company, Danbury Mint. Cookie Jar is 12" in height; platter is 14" in length, Set: $119 to $130

There were two sets of Funfetti items produced. The cookie jars look similar at first glance but, they have different traits. The first Funfetti set was produced in 1992. This cookie jar has the Doughboy's left hand behind his back, and his legs are crossed. The cupcake is larger and is tan on the bottom. The set that came out in 2001 has its own special characteristics. The Doughboy is standing straighter, his legs are not crossed, he is holding his left hand by his head, and the cupcake color is yellow. The 1992 set is harder to find as the set was discontinued when it was discovered that the pieces broke easily. You will see pieces of the Funfetti sets in other areas of this book, under salt and pepper shakers, utensil holders, etc. You will find their distinctions listed at those sites. Most pieces are marked with the year of manufacture.

Funfetti Cookie Jar. Item is marked on bottom. 2001 The Pillsbury Company, Benjamin & Medwin Inc. NY, NY. 12" in height, Made in China, $45 to $50

Doughboy Funfetti Cookie Jar. Item is marked on bottom. 1992 The Pillsbury Company, Benjamin & Medwin Inc. NY, NY. 9 1/2" in height, $55 to $60

Anchor Hocking Goodie Jar. This is a large clear glass jar designed to hold all kinds of goodies. This item is unmarked. 1991 The Pillsbury Company. 9 1/2" in height, $25 to $30

Chapter 3

Salt and Pepper Shakers

Plastic, glass, and ceramic salt and pepper shakers are illustrated. The hard to find Poppin & Poppie Range Set is described, which is larger in size yet very similar to the Poppin & Poppie salt and pepper shakers.

Doughboy Salt & Pepper Shakers. These salt and pepper shakers were offered as a promotional item. They are ceramic with blue paint applied after firing. The paint has a tendency to chip and come off easily with wear. It is hard to find these items in mint condition. Shakers are marked on bottom, but it is very difficult to make out what is printed. The Pillsbury Company, Imported from China. 3 1/2" in height. A set in the original box sold for $102.50 on E-bay. Most sets with some wear are selling for $45 to $55

Poppin & Poppie Salt & Pepper Shakers. The bases of these plastic salt and pepper shakers are marked with their names, and on the back of the base is the date they were produced. 1974 The Pillsbury Company, Poppin is 4" in height, Poppie is 3 1/2" in height. $38 to $45

Funfetti Salt & Pepper Shakers. This is the first set of Funfetti Salt and Pepper Shakers produced. This set is unmarked. Made in 1992 The Pillsbury Company, Benjamin & Medwin Inc NY, NY. Doughboy is 4" in height; Cupcake is 2 1/4" in height, $25 to $30

Funfetti Salt & Pepper Shaker. This is the later set of Funfetti Salt and Pepper Shakers. You might want to compare this set to the one made in 1992 to see the differences. The salt and pepper shakers are marked on the bottom: 2001 TPC Inc., B & M Inc. NY NY, Made in China. Doughboy is 5" in height; Cupcake is 2 1/4" in height, $14 to $20

Range Set. Poppin and Poppie Salt & Pepper Shakers. This range set is larger in size than the regular salt and pepper shakers that look like this set. The set is marked on bottom. 1988 The Pillsbury Company. Each is 5" in height, $50 to $60

Poppin and Poppie Salt & Pepper Shakers. This salt and pepper shakers look like the range set but are smaller in size. They are marked on bottom. 1988 The Pillsbury Company. Poppin has a sticker that reads: TPC 1988, Made in Taiwan. Each is 4" in height, $25 to $30

Doughboy Salt & Pepper Shakers. This salt and pepper shaker set has two Doughboys, each posing differently. Marked on the bottom: 1997 TPC Inc., B & M Inc. NY, NY, Made in China. Each is 4" in height, $18 to $25

Doughboy Baker Salt & Pepper Shakers. The set comes with the Doughboy and a flour sack. The flour sack is unmarked. The Doughboy is marked: 1997 TPC Inc., B & M Inc. NY, NY, Made in China. Doughboy is 4" in height; Flour sack is 3 1/4"in height, $18 to $25

Doughboy Salt & Pepper Shakers. The Doughboy and flour sack are much smaller in diameter than the other salt and pepper shakers. The flour sack is unmarked. The Doughboy is marked: B & M NY, 2002 TPC., China. Doughboy is 4" in height; Flour Bag is 3" in height, $8 to $15

Anchor Hocking Salt & Pepper Shakers. The Doughboy's portrait is on the front of these clear glass salt and pepper shakers. These salt and pepper shakers are unmarked. 1991 The Pillsbury Company. 5" in height, $28 to $35

Chapter 4

Kitchen Ware

Ceramics, porcelains, glass and plastics provide the materials for kitchen ware for practically every purpose with the Doughboy attending to every need.

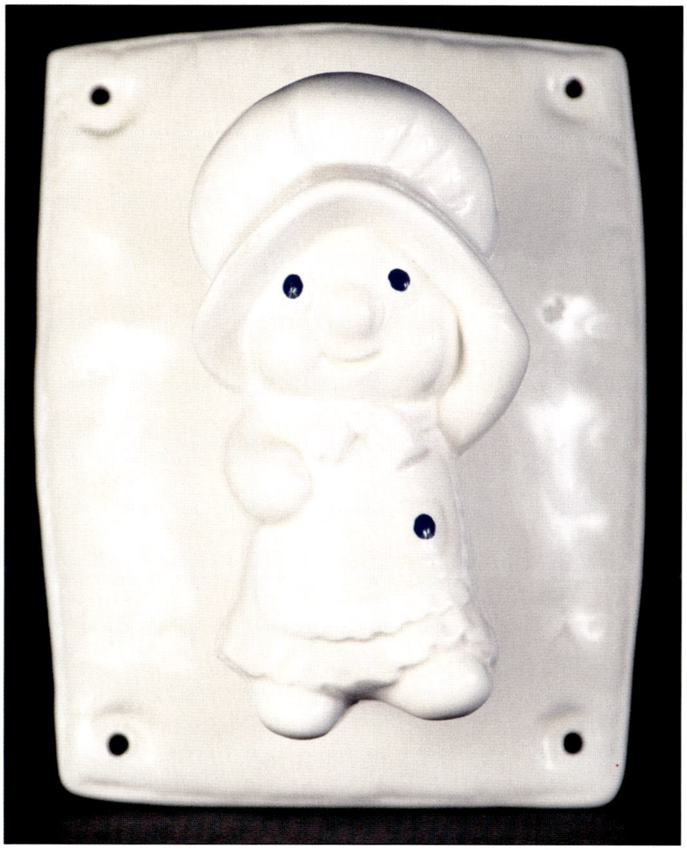

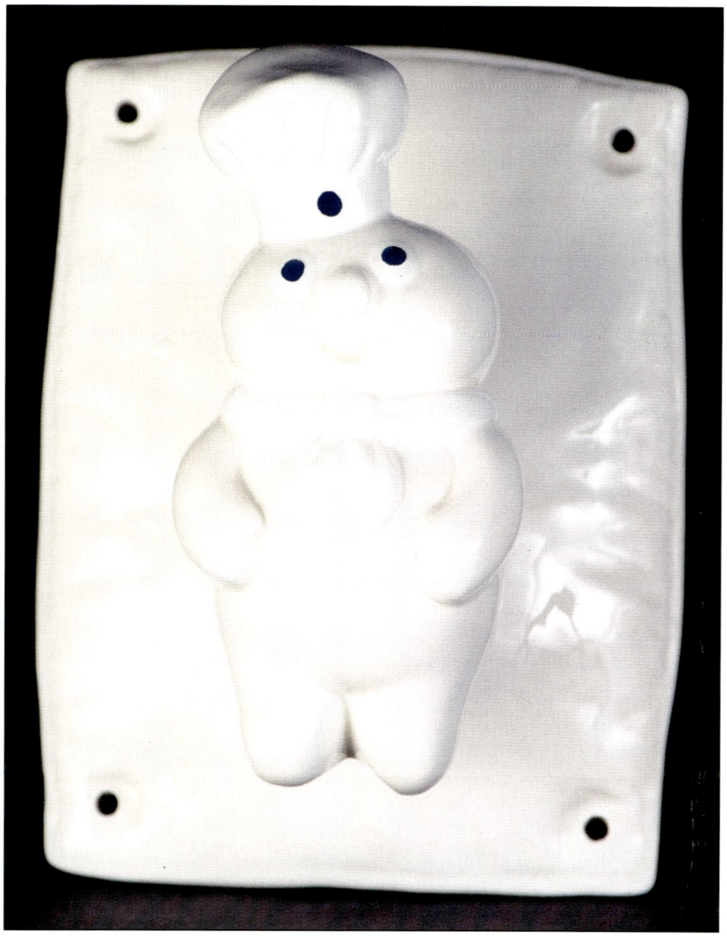

Pillsbury Towel Holders

Poppin and Poppie Towel Holder. These towel holders are unique. Poppin and Poppie are raised from the base 4 1/2" to form the hook to hang your towels. These towel holders are made of ceramic. The towel holders would be secured to the wall by screws. The towel holders are unmarked. 1988 The Pillsbury Company. Base is 7" by 5 1/4". Poppin Towel Holder \$55 to \$65; Poppie Towel Holder \$60 to \$70

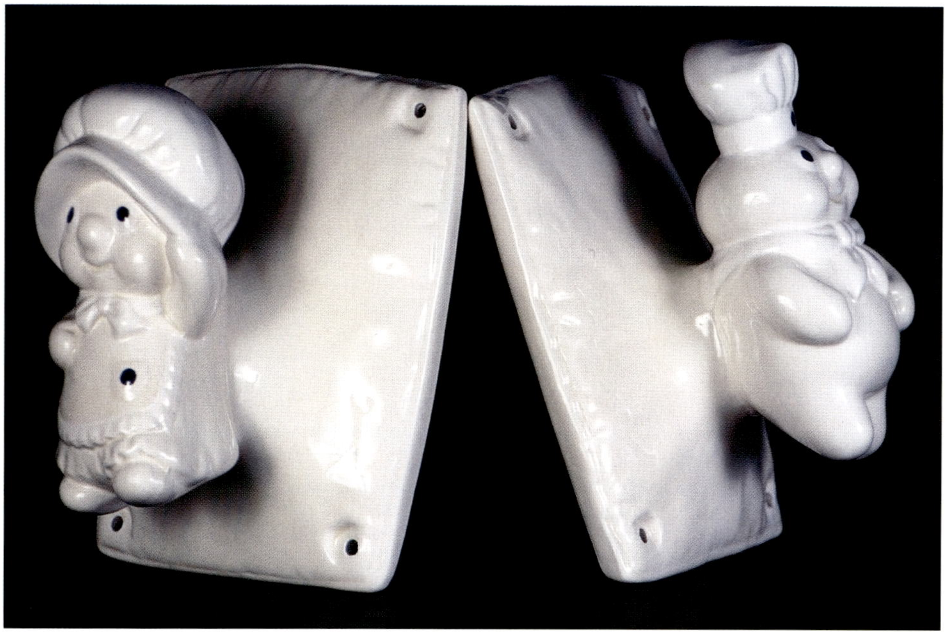

The Pillsbury Doughboy Porcelain Tea Set. It's time for tea, with this elegant porcelain tea set. The set is made of fine porcelain and trimmed with 23K gold. Each piece of this set has a unique picture of the Doughboy. On the tea pot the Doughboy is shown stirring a cup of tea. The sugar bowl has the Doughboy carrying a bag of sugar. The creamer has the Doughboy carrying milk. A numbered Certificate of Authenticity comes with this set. Each item is marked. 2003 The Pillsbury Company, Danbury Mint, Hand Crafted in China. The set includes: the tea pot, 5 1/4" tall by 9" wide, sugar bowl, 3 3/4" tall by 5" wide, and the creamer, 3 1/2" tall by 6 1/4" wide, $79 to $100

Doughboy Candlesticks. Your table will light up with this adorable set of candlesticks featuring the Doughboy holding a spoon and a fork. The Candlesticks come with a numbered Certificate of Authenticity. Candlesticks are marked. 2000 The Pillsbury Company, Danbury Mint. 6" in height, $78 to $90

Set of 3 Original Doughboy Mixing Bowls. Each bowl is white and is adorned with four raised Doughboys. Bowls are marked with a label. If used, the label may be gone or removed. 1988 The Pillsbury Company, Benjamin & Medwin, Inc., Made in Portugal. Bowls dimensions and capacities are: 8" diameter holds 1 1/2 quarts, 7" diameter holds 1 quart, 6" diameter holds 1/2 quart. $45 to $55 for set

Doughboy Baker Mixing Bowls. This set comes with 3 bowls. Bowls are adorned with four raised Baker Doughboys and have a blue trim around the top of each bowl. Bowls are marked on the bottom. 2000 The Pillsbury Company, Benjamin & Medwin Inc. NY, NY, Made in Thailand. Bowls dimensions and capacities are: 8" diameter holds 1 1/2 quarts, 7" diameter holds 1 quart, 6" diameter holds 1/2 quart. $35 to $45 for set

All American Boy Bowl Set. This set features the All American Boy pattern, represented with the Doughboy and apples. The color is red, white, and blue. The set comes with 3 steel bowls with plastic covers. Bowls are marked on bottom. 2000 The Pillsbury Company, Reston Lloyd Ltd. Bowls are 1 3/4 qt., 1 1/4 qt, 3/4 qt. $15 to $25 for set

Chef Bowl Set. Set contains 3 steel bowls with plastic lids in the Chef design, which features the Doughboy on a blue diamond. There are blue diamonds on each side of the Doughboy with a chef hat in each one. Bowls are marked on the bottom. 2000 The Pillsbury Company, Reston Lloyd Ltd. Bowls are 1 3/4 qt, 1 1/4 qt, 3/4 qt. $15 to $25 for set

Anchor Ovenware Mixing Bowl Set. These glass bowls show the Doughboy holding a spoon, appearing next to the Doughboy in red is his name "Poppin Fresh". A checkered blue and white pattern accents each bowl. Each bowls feature Home Cookin' by displaying the word "home" above and "cookin" below the checkered pattern. Bowls are marked with maker, size, "oven and microwave safe" and "no stove top or broiler use". These items are often sold separately. Bowls do not show the date manufactured. 1991 The Pillsbury Company. Comes with a 1 1/2qt. bowl, $12 to $25, and a 1 qt. bowl, $8 to $18

Anchor Ovenware 2 Cup Measuring Cup. A full size picture of the Doughboy holding a spoon appears on this 2 cup glass measuring cup. Appearing next to the Doughboy in red is his name "Poppin Fresh". Measuring cup is microwave safe. The year does not appear on the measuring cup. 1991 The Pillsbury Company. $25 to $30

Anchor Ovenware 1 1/2qt. Casserole Dish with lid. The glass casserole dish shows the Doughboy holding a spoon, appearing next to the Doughboy in red is his name "Poppin Fresh". A checkered blue and white pattern accents the casserole dish. The casserole dish feature Home Cookin' by displaying the word "home" above and "cookin" below the checkered pattern. Casserole dish is marked with maker, size, "oven and microwave safe" and "not for stove or broiler use". The year does not appear on casserole dish. 1991 The Pillsbury Company. $25 to $35

Anchor Ovenware Baking Dish. This glass baking dish is in the same design as the previous Anchor Ovenware. It shows the Doughboy holding a spoon, appearing next to the Doughboy in red is his name "Poppin Fresh". A checkered blue and white pattern accents the baking dish. This baking dish features Home Cookin' by displaying the word "home" above and "cookin" below the checkered pattern. Baking dish is marked with maker, size, "oven and microwave safe" and "not for stove or broiler use". 1991 The Pillsbury Company, 8" x 8" x 2", $18 to $23

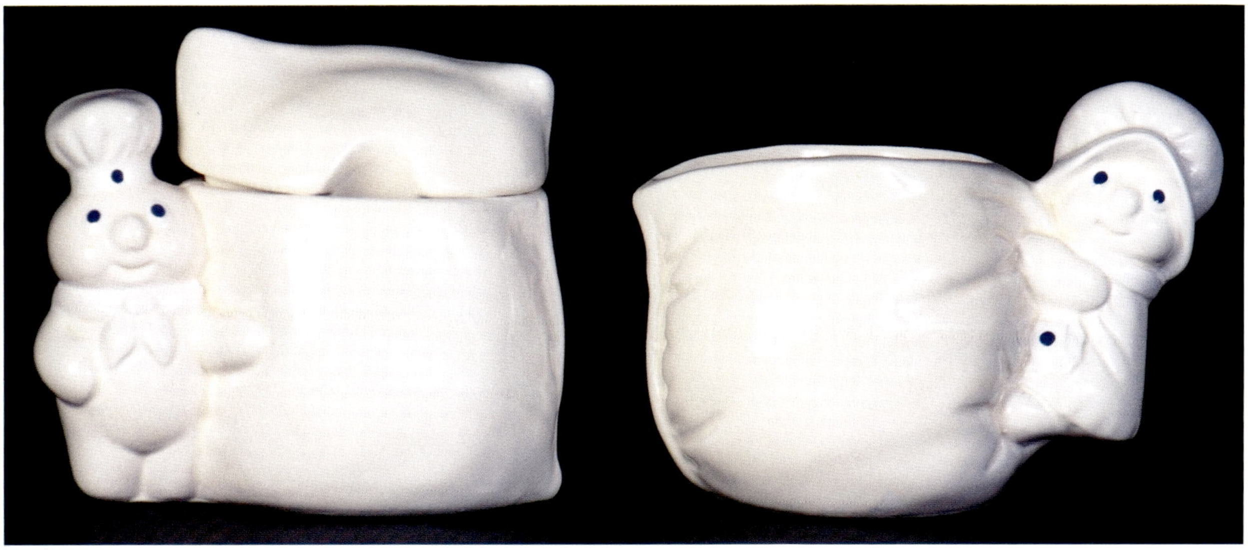

Poppin Sugar & Poppie Creamer. Poppin and Poppie make adorable handles for this sugar and creamer set. Each piece is marked on the bottom. 1988 TPC (The Pillsbury Company), sticker: Made in Taiwan. 3" in height, $35 to $45

Doughboy Baker Cream & Sugar. The Doughboy is holding a plate of cookies on the creamer from the Baker series. The sugar has a lid with an opening for a spoon. The Doughboy on the sugar is holding a coffee mug. Both pieces are marked on bottom. 1999 The Pillsbury Company, Benjamin & Medwin Inc. NY, NY, Made in China. 4" in height, $28 to $35

Doughboy Sugar and Creamer. The Doughboy sits beside this sugar bowl. The sugar bowl came with a plastic spoon when sold originally. Sugar bowl is unmarked. Creamer is marked: 2002 The Pillsbury Company, Benjamin & Medwin Inc., Made in China. Creamer: 3" in height, Sugar: 3 1/2" x 4" in height, $10 to $15

Doughboy Napkin Holder. This piece presents Poppin standing in front of two sacks of flour. If you look on the back you will find embossed in the ceramic material the word "flour" on each bag. Piece is marked on bottom. 1988 The Pillsbury Company, Benjamin & Medwin Inc. NY, NY, Made in China. 5" wide x 5" in height $26 to $30

Funfetti Napkin Holder. The Doughboy is standing in front of the Funfetti cupcake. This piece is of the older of the Funfetti sets. The new set produced in 2001 did not come with a napkin holder. Napkin holder is unmarked. 1992 The Pillsbury Company, Benjamin & Medwin Inc. NY, NY. 4 1/4" wide x 5" in height, $30 to $35

Doughboy Napkin Holder. As all of the 2002 series this napkin holder is smaller in size. It has an attractive Doughboy on the front of the napkin holder. Napkin holder is marked on the bottom. 2002 The Pillsbury Company, Benjamin & Medwin, Inc., Made in China. 3 1/2" wide x 3 1/2" in height, $8 to $12

Doughboy Baker Scouring Pad Holder. As all of the Baker Series this pad holder has the Doughboy holding a plate of cookies. Marked on bottom: 1997 The Pillsbury Company, Benjamin & Medwin Inc. NY, NY, Made in China. 4 1/4" in height, $20 to $25

Funfetti Scouring Pad Holder. This is a delightful scouring pad holder. It is designed to store the scouring pad in the back of the cupcake. Marked on bottom. 2001 The Pillsbury Company, Benjamin & Medwin NY, NY, Made in China. 5" in height, $18 to $20

Doughboy Scouring Pad Holder. The Doughboy sits at the side of the scouring pad holder. The holder is very small so the pad only goes half way. Marked on bottom. 2002 The Pillsbury Company, Benjamin & Medwin, Inc., Made in China. 5" wide x 4" in height, $8 to $12

Doughboy Baker Utensil Holder. The Baker Doughboy is holding a plate of cookies. The utensils which came with this holder are stored behind the Doughboy. Marked on the bottom. 1997 The Pillsbury Company, Benjamin & Medwin Inc. NY, NY, Made in China. 8" in height, $25 to $30

Funfetti Utensil Holder. The Doughboy looks as if he is waving to you as he stands beside the cupcake. The cupcake holds the utensils that came with this set. Utensil holder is marked: 2001 The Pillsbury Company, Benjamin & Medwin NY, NY, Made in China. 8" in height, $22 to $25

Funfetti Utensil Holder. The Doughboy stands at the side of the cupcake which holds the utensils. The item is marked. 1992 The Pillsbury Company, Benjamin & Medwin Inc. NY, NY, Made in Taiwan. 8" in height, $30 to $40

Funfetti Spoon Rest. The Doughboy stands beside a cupcake each is designed to hold a spoon. This item is marked. 2001 The Pillsbury Company, Benjamin & Medwin NY, NY, Made in China. 7" in height, $15 to $20

Poppin & Poppie Spoon Rest. Poppin and Poppie together help in the kitchen by holding your spoons. The spoon rest is marked on the bottom. 1997 The Pillsbury Company, Benjamin & Medwin Inc. NY, NY, Made in China. 6 3/4" in height x 5 3/4" wide, $26 to $35

Doughboy Spoon Rest. The Doughboy with hands at his sides is designed to hold a spoon. This item is marked on the bottom. 1988 The Pillsbury Company, Benjamin & Medwin Inc. NY, NY, Made in China. 8" in height, $18 to $25

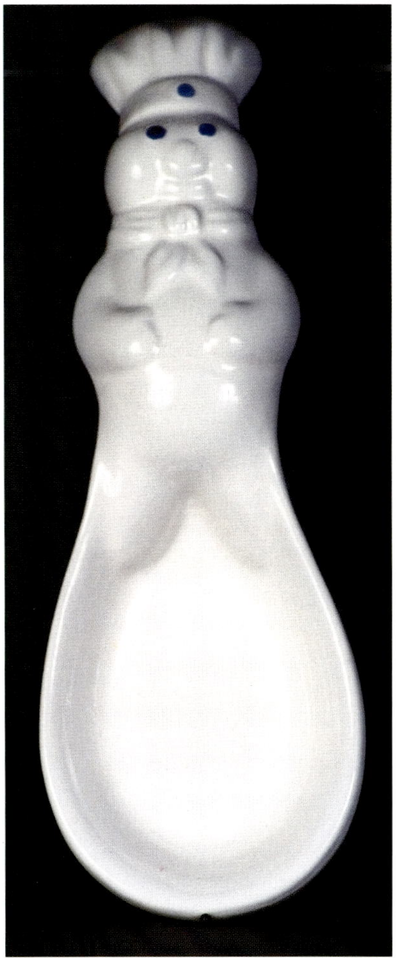

Doughboy Spoon Rest. The Doughboy has been crafted to be the handle of this unique spoon rest. The spoon rest is marked on the bottom. 2002 The Pillsbury Company, Benjamin & Medwin Inc. NY, NY. 7 3/4" long x 2 3/4"wide, $6 to $12

Melamine Chef Spoon Rest. The Doughboy is featured in this spoon rest with a blue diamond shape behind him. This item is not marked with the year manufactured unless the tag is still attached. 2000 The Pillsbury Company, Made by Reston Lloyd LTD. 8" in height, $8 to $15

Chef Tea Kettle (Metal). The tea kettle has the Doughboy imprinted on a blue diamond. On each side of the Doughboy a chef's hat is shown inside a smaller blue diamond. The kettle is marked on the bottom. 1999 The Pillsbury Company, Reston Lloyd LTD. 9" to top of handle, $25 to $35

All American Tea Kettle (Metal). All American Tea Kettle displays the Doughboy in a blue square with stars around him. There is a square on either side, one picturing apples and the other a pie. This kettle is marked on the bottom, 1999 The Pillsbury Company, Reston Lloyd LTD. 2 qt. tea kettle, 7" in diameter, $20 to $30

Doughboy Baker Tea Pot. An adorable ceramic tea pot with a long spout features the Doughboy with a plate of cookies. The Doughboy is ready to pour you some tea for your afternoon snack or anytime. This tea pot is marked on the bottom. 1997 The Pillsbury Company, Benjamin & Medwin Inc. NY, NY. Made in China, 8" in height, $55 to $65

Doughboy Baker Butter Spreaders. The adorable Doughboy is the perfect handle for these unique butter spreaders. Set includes four spreaders. Spreaders are not marked. 1999 The Pillsbury Company, Benjamin & Medwin Inc. NY, NY. 5" Knife & Handle, $15 to $20

Doughboy Baker Pitcher. The Doughboy's chef hat forms a pouring spout for this ceramic pitcher and a large handle makes the pitcher easy to hold. The pitcher is marked on the bottom. 1999 The Pillsbury Company, Benjamin & Medwin Inc. NY, NY, Made in China. 8 3/4" in height, $45 to $55

Doughboy Baker Trivet. The ceramic trivet has a blue boarder with the Doughboy standing beside a bag of cookies. The trivet is marked on the bottom. 1999 The Pillsbury Company, Benjamin & Medwin Inc. NY, NY, Made in China. 6 1/2" square, $20 to $25

Doughboy Baker Platter. The Doughboy is featured sitting at the top of this large platter waiting to hold your goodies. The platter is marked on the bottom. 1999 The Pillsbury Company, Benjamin & Medwin Inc. NY, NY, Made in China. 12" Circular Platter, Doughboy is 4" in height. $35 to $40

Chef Doughboy Trivet. The Doughboy is imprinted on a blue diamond. On each side of the Doughboy a chef's hat is shown inside a smaller blue diamond. The trivet is made of Melamine. Manufactured date is located on box. 2000 The Pillsbury Company. Trivet is marked on the bottom: Reston Lloyd LTD. 8" in diameter, $8 to $13

Doughboy Cookie Stamp. The raised figures and items displayed on the top of this cookie stamp make's it decorative. Around the base of the cookie stamp it displays the saying "Nothin' says lovin' like something from the oven". The finished cookie will display the Doughboy holding a rolling pin (bottom of cookie stamp shown in the second picture). A recipe for "Stamped Shortbread Cookies" came with the stamp. The stamp is not marked. 1998 The Pillsbury Company, Creative Imaginations Inc., Made in China. 5" in height, $15 to $20

Doughboy Cookie Cutter. Make cut out cookies of the Doughboy with this cookie cutter, which has a round handle attached to make it easy to hold. The cookie cutter is unmarked. 1997 The Pillsbury Company. 3 1/4" in height, $7 to $10

Cookie Cutters. This is a set of 4 cookie cutters each one has the Doughboy on the top in a different pose. The cutters come in the shape of a moon, star, heart, and diamond. The cookie cutters are made of a hard plastic material. 1992 The Pillsbury Company. $10 to $15

Doughboy Metal Mold with finished plastic example. Items are unmarked. 5" in height, $15 to $20

Doughboy Stainless Flatware. The Doughboy can grow up with your child with this 6 piece growth set that comes with an infant spoon, toddler spoon and fork, preschool fork, spoon, and knife. Each piece features the Doughboy on the handle (close up photo shown). Made in the USA by Oneida®. $30 to $35

14 Piece Utensil Set. Set includes: jumbo spatula, jumbo scraper, set of 4 measuring cups, set of 5 measuring spoons, 10" whisk and a pastry brush. Each utensil has a comfort-grip handle with a picture of the doughboy on the front of the piece, except the measuring cups and spoons. Since they stack together the Doughboy appears only on the top item, which is the 1/8 measuring cup and the just a pinch measuring spoon. The utensils are marked: China. The year produced would have to be obtained from the box. 2000 The Pillsbury Company, Lifetime Hoan Corp. $20 to $25

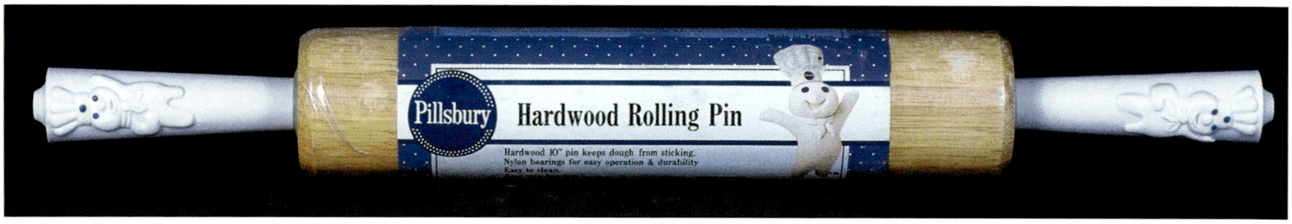

Doughboy Hardwood Rolling Pin. This hardwood rolling pin has a raised Doughboy on each handle. Marked on lower part of handle. 1991 TPC, Lifetime Hoan Corp., 17 1/4" long, $20 to $30

Doughboy Pizza Cutter. This pizza cutter has a raised Doughboy on the handle. It is in its original package and the back can not be observed to see if item is marked. Package is marked: 1992 The Pillsbury Company. 4 1/2" Handle, 2 3/4" circular blade, $12 to $18

Two-Piece Spatula Set. Set comes with two differently shaped scrapers. A raised Doughboy is on each handle. Spatulas are in original packaging unable to see if they are individually marked. Package is marked: 1996 The Pillsbury Company. Lifetime Hoan Corporation, The spatulas are 9 3/4" long and 9 1/2" long, $8 to $12 per set

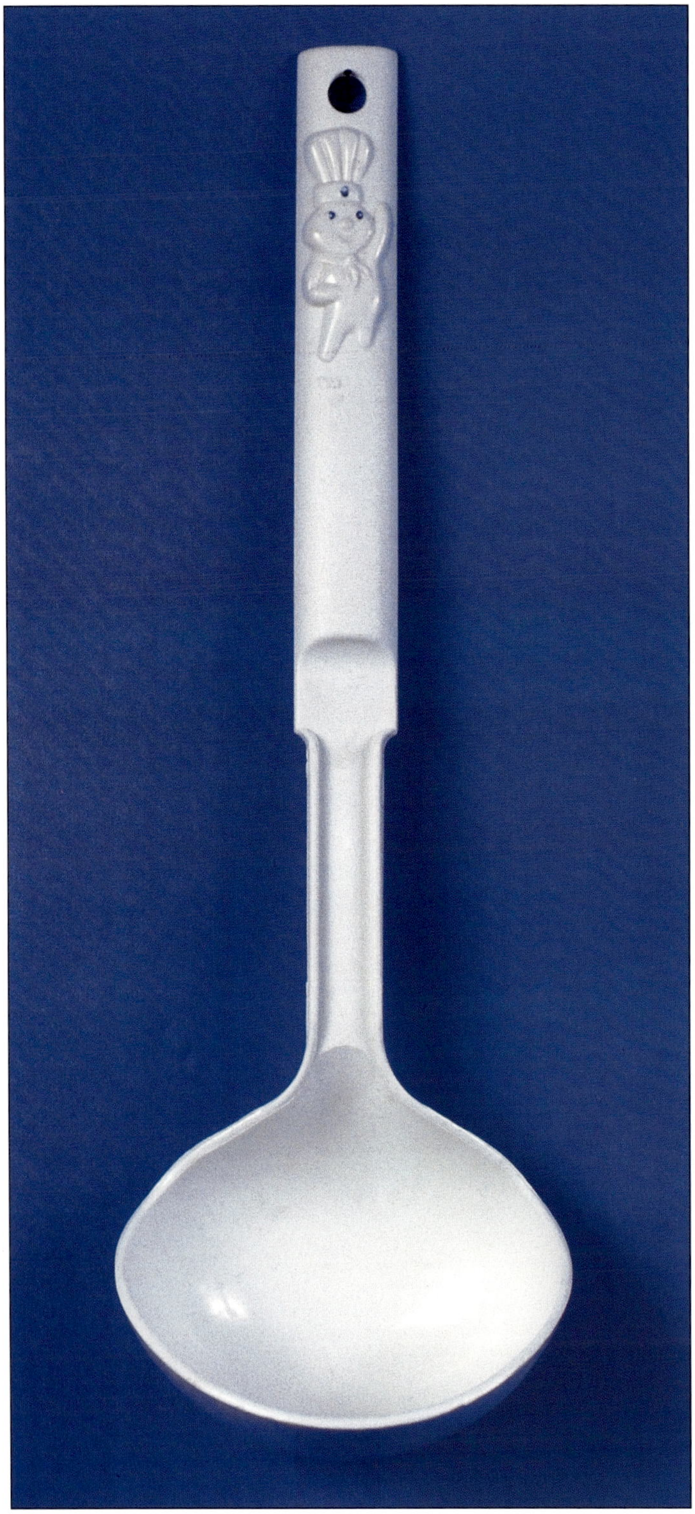

Doughboy Ladle. The raised Doughboy on this handle looks like he is waving to you. The back of the handle is marked: 1993 TPC, Malaysia. 9" Handle $15 to $18

Dough Scraper. This dough scraper has a raised Doughboy on the handle holding a rolling pin. The dough scraper has a stainless steel blade and easy-grip handle to make clean-ups easier. The dough scraper is dishwasher safe. The date can be found on package: 1992 The Pillsbury Company. 6 1/2" Handle, 6" x 3" scrapper, $12 to $15

Doughboy Pancake Ring. Let the Doughboy help make all your pancakes the same size. You can also use the pancake ring to make your fried eggs perfectly round. Pancake ring is unmarked. 1992 The Pillsbury Company, Lifetime Hoan Corp. 4 3/4" Circular, 2" Doughboy on handle, $9 to $15

Large Bag Clip. The bag clip has the Doughboy holding a bag of groceries and an ear of corn. The Doughboy could help you keep your snacks fresh longer or keep your favorite recipes clipped together. Bag clip is marked: 1992 TPC, China. The package is marked: 1992 The Pillsbury Company, Lifetime Hoan Corp. Plastic, 5 3/8" wide x 3 1/2" tall, $8 to $12

General Mills/Pillsbury Bag Clip. This item was one of several made to promote General Mills and The Pillsbury Company merger it features the Doughboy holding a "G" for General Mills. Bag Clip is made of lightweight plastic and is unmarked. 4" wide, $5 to $10

Pillsbury Recycle Bag Holder. This cloth Doughboy bag holder has a strap for easy hanging, and for easy insertion of the bags Velcro has been placed in the back seam, when a bag is needed just pull it out from the bottom. Item is marked. 2003 The Pillsbury Company, Global Innovations, LLC, Made in China. 16 1/2" by 8", $10 to $15

Pillsbury Doughboy Timer. The Doughboy is so adorable standing atop this one hour kitchen timer. This timer was purchased from Germany. There are no markings on the timer to substantiate its validity. 4 1/2" in height, $25 to $35

Doughboy Plastic Cup. This cup is a wonderful replica of the Doughboy. With his hands on his stomach it looks like he's been giggling – "Hoo Hoo!". Marked on the back under the rim: 1979 The Pillsbury Company, made in the USA, 4 1/2" in height x 2 3/4" across top, $10 to $15

Pillsbury Cookie and Cow Cup. The Doughboy is riding a cow on this cup which was made in the 1970s. This insulated cup is made of plastic and marked on the bottom: Made in the USA, Thermo-Serv a Division of West Bend. 4" in height 10 oz., $15 to $25

Doughboy Cup. Made of a ceramic material, the cup has a blue background with small white Doughboys scattered around the cup. On the front of the cup there is one large Blue Doughboy, until you add hot liquid. Like "magic" the Doughboy turns white. This cup was purchased from Germany. There are no markings on the cup to substantiate its validity. 3 3/4" in height, $35 to $40

On Parade Cup. The Doughboy is having his own parade marching around the cup playing his tuba, drums, and other instruments. The Pillsbury Company, 1991, is printed on the cup, located by the handle under the Doughboy playing a drum. There are no other markings on the cup. Manufactured by, Corelle® by Corning. 3 1/2" in height, $12 to $17

On Parade Plate. The Doughboy marches to his own music as he circles the plate. The plate is marked on the back: 1991 The Pillsbury Company, Corelle® by Corning. 10" in diameter, $25 to $30

On Parade Glass. The Doughboy is marching around this plastic glass. The Pillsbury Company, 1991, is printed on the glass, located under the Doughboy playing a drum. There are no other markings on the glass. Manufactured by, Corelle® by Corning. 5" tall, $9 to $15

Limited-Edition Collector Plate, Ingredients for Fun, Hand Painted by Bill Bell. This plate captures the detail and charm of the Doughboy as he stands on a flour tin with all of the ingredients he needs for fun in the kitchen. The gold trim on the plate makes it look elegant. This plate comes with a numbered Certificate of Authenticity. The plate is marked on the back: 2000 The Pillsbury Company, Danbury Mint. 8" in diameter, $45 to $55

Doughboy 30th Birthday! Collector Glass. This glass was made for the Doughboy's 30th birthday. The box has information on it about the Doughboy. The glass is marked October 1995. 1995 The Pillsbury Company. 5 1/2" tall, $12 to $18

Pillsbury Doughboy Canisters. This delightful 3-D canister set is sure to add some fun to your kitchen. The 4 piece canister set is made of glazed ceramic and is showing the Doughboy doing what he does best, helping you prepare your favorite recipe. As a special touch the Doughboy's chef hat is used for the handles on the canister set. A Certificate of Authenticity comes with the canister set. Marked on the bottom: 2001 The Pillsbury Company, Danbury Mint. Canisters range in size from 7 3/4" to 11" in height, Set: $119 to $129

Pillsbury Doughboy Cookie Jar & Cookie Platter. These two items are sold as a set. Whether you're serving cookies to friends or family, this set is sure to delight everyone. The 3-D Cookie jar pictures the Doughboy holding one of his favorite cookies. An assortment of cookies surrounds the platter with the Doughboy embossed in the center to lend a hand. A numbered Certificate of Authenticity comes with this set. The set is marked on the bottom. 2002 The Pillsbury Company, Danbury Mint. Cookie Jar is 12" in height; platter is 14" in length, Set: $119 to $130

Chapter 5

Soap and Lotion Dispensers

Let the Doughboy hold your soap or lotion in these decorative dispensers.

Doughboy Soap Dish. The cute little Doughboy sits in the corner of this ceramic soap dish ready to hold your bar of soap. The soap dish is unmarked. 4 1/2" x 4", $35 to $45

Doughboy Soap/Lotion Dispenser. This Doughboy can be used as a soap or lotion dispenser. The dispenser is marked on the bottom: 1997 The Pillsbury Company, Benjamin & Medwin NY, NY, Made in China. 8" in height, $18 to $25

Funfetti Soap/Lotion Dispenser. The Funfetti soap/lotion dispenser with its colorful cupcake is sure to bring a smile to your face each time you use it. Dispenser is marked on the bottom: 2001 The Pillsbury Company, Benjamin & Medwin NY, NY, Made in China, 7" in height, $18 to $24

Doughboy Soap/Lotion Dispenser. This soap/lotion dispenser has a raised Doughboy on the front. Dispenser is marked on the bottom: 1988 The Pillsbury Company, 6" in height, $23 to $30

Doughboy Baker Soap/Lotion Dispenser. The Doughboy always wants to help and this is no exception. This dispenser can be filled with your favorite soap or lotion. The dispenser is marked on the bottom: 1997 The Pillsbury Company, Benjamin & Medwin NY, NY, Made in China. 8" in height, $18 to $24

Chef Doughboy Soap Dispenser. This Doughboy soap dispenser will bring some color to your kitchen with his red checkered mitts. 2003 The Pillsbury Company, Benjamin and Medwin, 8 1/2" in height, $10 to $20

Chapter 6

Banks

The Doughboy can help you save money in the banks made of cast iron, ceramic, and plastic. The cast iron bank is animated, pull down the Doughboy's hand and he rolls the coin in the oven. When you drop your coin in the giggle bank you will hear the Doughboy giggle "Hoo Hoo!".

Doughboy Cast Iron Mechanical Bank, Limited Edition. Let the Doughboy make saving money fun with this animated cast iron mechanical bank. When you push the Doughboy's left hand down, his right hand rolls the coin into an oven. The white oven has the Pillsbury logo on the side and a pan of cookies cooling on the top. The bank is marked on the bottom: 1998 The Pillsbury Company, China. 7" long by 2 5/8" wide, $55 to $65

Doughboy Giggle Bank. The Doughboy is standing on top of a green safe. The safe has a slot behind the Doughboy to drop coins in. Every time you drop some money in the bank the Doughboy giggles—"Hoo Hoo!". The bank is marked on the back: 1999 The Pillsbury Company, Made in China. 9" in height, $25 to $30

Doughboy Bank. The plastic Doughboy bank will hold coins for you. The coins are inserted in the slot on the Doughboy's back. A stopper on the bottom of the bank makes it easy to remove the coins. The bank is unmarked. If tag is still attached you can locate the following: 1998 The Pillsbury Company, Fun 4 All Corp. 11" in height, $18 to $25

Doughboy Ceramic Bank. This Doughboy is standing tall to hold your coins. The coin is inserted in the back of the Doughboy's head and a stopper in the bottom makes it easy to remove the coin without breaking the bank. The bank is marked on the bottom; 1985 The Pillsbury Company, 7" in height, $25 to $30

Doughboy Large Ceramic Bank. The Doughboy is making it easy for you to save, with a slit in the back of his head to drop your coins into this large ceramic bank. Take the stopper out of the bottom of the bank to remove your coins. The bank is marked on the bottom: 1988 The Pillsbury Company, Made in Taiwan. 8" in height, $25 to $35

Chapter 7

Linens and Rugs

Items are grouped in their matching sets. Sets include Poppin Fresh, All American Boy, Holiday Bake Off, and the Doughboy pocket line. These sets feature different colors from the Poppin Fresh line done in blues and whites to the All American Boy line done in red, white, and blue.

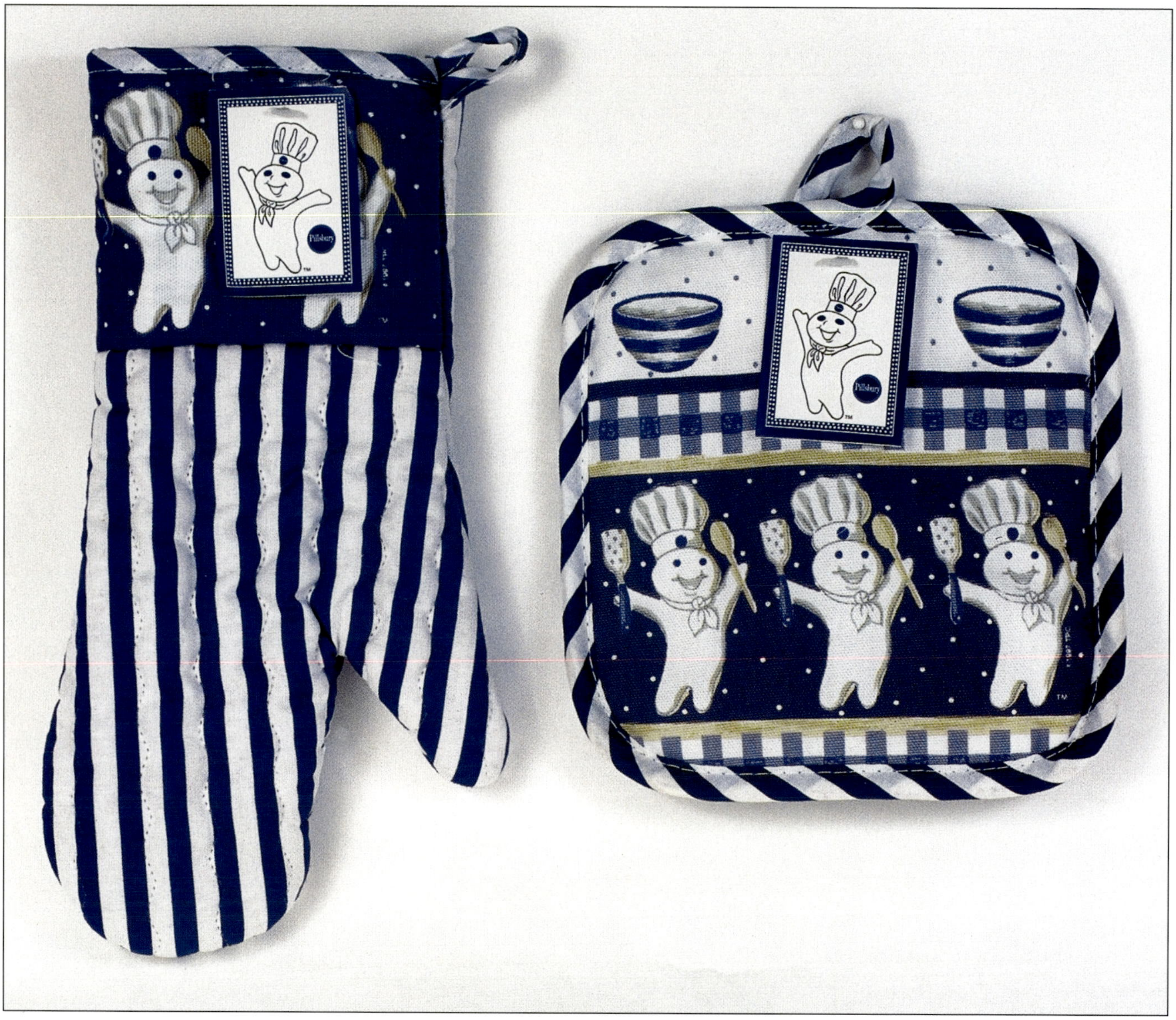

Poppin Fresh Pot Holder & Mitt. Doughboys circle the top of this blue and white striped mitt holding a spoon in one hand and a spatula in the other. There is a matching pot holder, each are sold separately. The checkered and striped pot holder has three Doughboys across the bottom and three mixing bowls across the top. The pot holder and mitt are unmarked. 1997 The Pillsbury Company, Barth & Dreyfuss of California. Mitt $10 to $15, Pot Holder $8 to $10

Poppin Fresh Rug. The Doughboy is shown across the rug holding a spoon and a spatula one in each hand. Mitts, bowls, and utensils are displayed below the Doughboy. The rug has a blue and white checkered design on the top and bottom. The rug is marked: 1997 The Pillsbury Company. Glenoit NY, NY, 18" x 30", $40 to $50

Poppin Fresh Tie-Up Towel. The Doughboy holding a spoon and spatula is displayed across the towel. Mitts, bowls, and utensils are displayed below the Doughboy. The blue and white striped cotton tie makes it easy to hang this terry towel anywhere. Towel is unmarked. 1997 The Pillsbury Company, Barth & Dreyfuss of California, Made in Indonesia. 15 1/2", $13 to $18

Poppin Fresh Cloth Place Mat. The place mat has a blue and white checkered pattern at the top and bottom. There are six Doughboys shown across the center of this place mat each holding a spoon and spatula, one in each hand. Above the Doughboy is a row of bowls and below are bowls, utensils, and mitts. The place mat has a short fringe around the mat. The mat is marked on the right side next to the Doughboy: 1997 TPC. 1997 The Pillsbury Company, Barth & Dreyfuss of California. 17 3/4" x 13 3/4", $5 to $10

Poppin Fresh Hand Towel. Blue and white terry hand towel features the Doughboy across the towel, with mixing bowls, mitts, and utensils. The towel is marked. 1997 The Pillsbury Company, Barth & Dreyfuss of California, Made in Mexico. 15" wide x 21" long, $9 to $14

Poppin Fresh Vinyl Place Mat. The Doughboy place mats will brighten up any table with its blue and white checkered design and the Doughboys across the middle of the mat. The place mat is marked on the right side next to the Doughboy; 1997 TPC. 1997 The Pillsbury Company, Barth & Dreyfuss of California. 17 3/4" x 11 3/4", $4 to $8

Poppin Fresh Vinyl Tablecloth, Flannel Back. Scattered across this blue and white checkered tablecloth is the Doughboy holding a spoon in one hand and a spatula in the other. Also, scattered on the tablecloth are bowls, rolling pins, and spoons. Package is marked: 1998 The Pillsbury Company, Barth & Dreyfuss of California. 52" x 70", $15 to $20

All American Boy Pot Holder & Mitt. The Doughboy is shown holding a spoon in the center of this red, white, and blue pot holder. There are apples behind him, and in front is an apple pie. The mitt has the Doughboy holding a spoon and beside him are a rolling pin and a bag of flour. Each sold separately. Items are marked on the right side next to the Doughboy: TPC 1998. 1998 The Pillsbury Company, Barth & Dreyfuss of California. Mitt $10 to $15, Pot Holder $8 to $10

All American Boy Rug. The rug is bordered by a red checked band. Six squares are shown on the rug. In three of the squares is the Doughboy. In the other squares you will find apples, a bag of flour with a rolling pin, and an apple pie. The rug has a rubber backing to prevent it from slipping. The rug is marked in the apple square: 1998 TPC. 1998 The Pillsbury Company, Glenoit NY. 18" x 30", $50 to $60

All American Boy Hand Towel. On the hand towel squares display the Doughboy, apples, a flour bag with a rolling pin, and an apple pie. This hand towel would go great with the matching dish towel. Towel is marked in the corner: 1998 TPC. 1998 The Pillsbury Company, Barth & Dreyfuss of California. 16" x 26", $6 to $10

All American Boy Dish Towel. On the dish towel squares display the Doughboy, apples, a flour bag with a rolling pin, and an apple pie. This dish towel would make a great companion for the matching hand towel shown. This dish towel is marked in the corner; TPC 1998. 1998 The Pillsbury Company, Barth & Dreyfuss of California. 12" x 12", $5 to $10

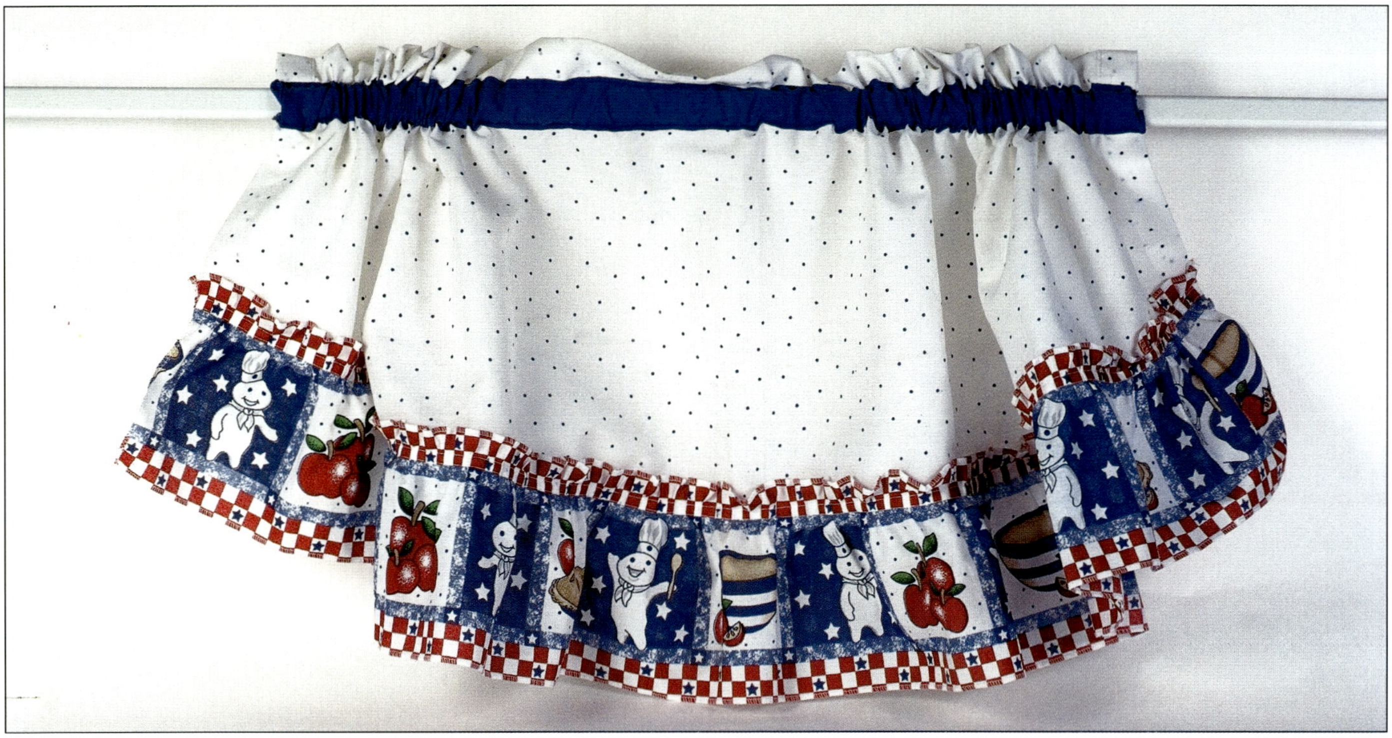

All American Boy Valance. The cotton valance are white with small blue polka dots, across the bottom are squares that display the Doughboy, a bowl, apples, and an apple pie. Center is 16" long by 48" wide. $25 to $35

Holiday Bake Off Pot Holder & Mitt. The pot holder and mitt are adorned with different shaped cut out cookies, featuring the Doughboy across the center, with colorful mitts, and holding a cookie. Each sold separately. Items are marked on the lower right side: 1999 TPC. 1999 The Pillsbury Company, Barth & Dreyfuss of California. Mitt $10 to $15, Pot Holder $8 to $10

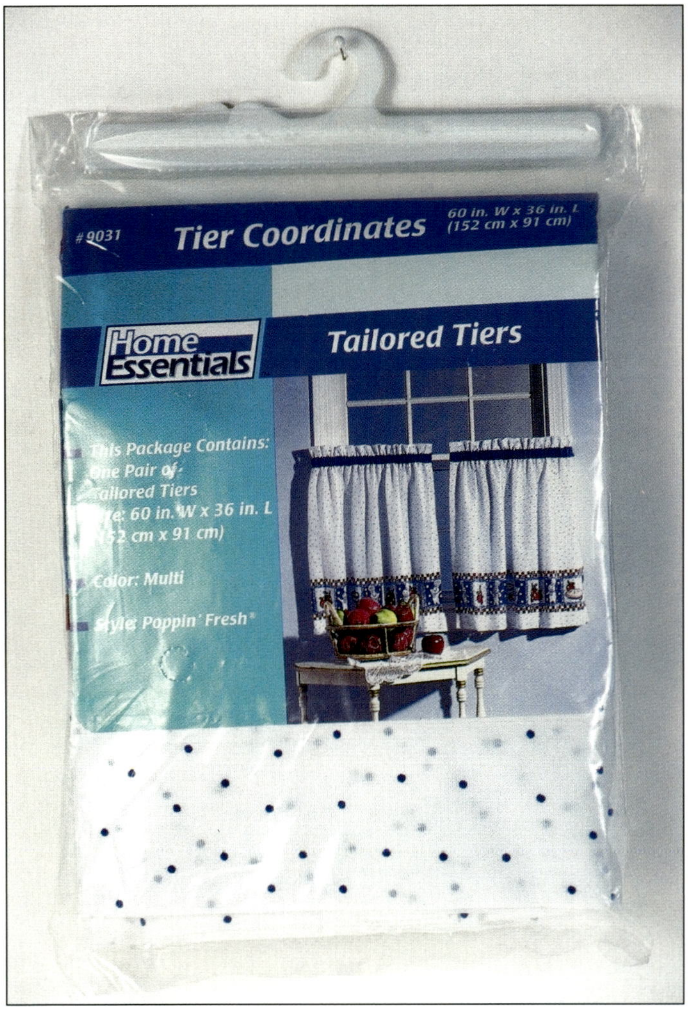

All American Boy Tailored Tiers. The cotton curtains are white with small blue polka dots, across the bottom are squares that display the Doughboy, a bowl, apples, and an apple pie. The package is marked: 1998 The Pillsbury Company, Made for K-Mart. 60" W x 36" L, $55 to $65

Holiday Bake Off Hand Towel. The Doughboy is shown with colorful mitts holding cookies with stars, hearts, and candy canes. There is a matching dish towel shown. Towel is marked: TPC 1999. 1999 The Pillsbury Company, Barth & Dreyfuss of California. 16" x 26", $6 to $12

Holiday Bake Off Dish Towel. The dish towel has the Doughboy in colorful mitts holding different shaped cookies. There is a matching hand towel shown. Dish towel is marked in corner: TPC 1999. 1999 The Pillsbury Company, Barth & Dreyfuss of California. 12" x 12", $5 to $10

Doughboy Pocket Apron. The apron is made of cotton material. The white Doughboy is appliqué to the blue material and fine detailing has been applied to form the eyes, mouth, and scarf. The Doughboy appears to be popping out of the large pocket at the bottom of the apron. Marked on label: 1997 The Pillsbury Company, Benjamin & Medwin Inc. 31 1/2" long x 27" wide, pocket is 10" wide x 7" deep, $25 to $30

Doughboy Pocket Pot Holder & Mitt. The pot holder and mitt is made of cotton material. The white Doughboy is appliqué to the blue material and fine detailing has been applied to form the eyes, mouth, and scarf. The matching mitt and pot holder are sold separately. They would make a nice matching set to your Doughboy Pocket Apron. Item is marked on the attached tag: 1997 The Pillsbury Company, Benjamin & Medwin, Inc. NY, NY. Mitt $12 to $18, Pot Holder $10 to $12

Chapter 8

Magnets

The Doughboy is stirring, baking, lying, and setting in this group of magnets. The Doughboy can even help you remember to get your goodies out of the oven with a magnet timer.

Doughboy Baker Magnet. The Doughboy serves his freshly baked bread on a raised plate. The magnet is marked with a sticker: 1998 The Pillsbury Company. 3" in height, $5 to $8

Doughboy Holding Cookie. The Doughboy is eating one of his favorite cookies. The magnet is marked with a sticker: 1998 The Pillsbury Company. 3" in height, $5 to $8

Doughboy on Flour Sack. The Doughboy is resting on a bag of flour. Marked by a sticker: 2000 The Pillsbury Company, Benjamin & Medwin NY, NY, Made in China, 2 1/2" in height, $5 to $8

Doughboy Making Cookies. The Doughboy has all of his ingredients to mix up his favorite cookies. Marked with a sticker: 1998 The Pillsbury Company. 3" in height, $5 to $8

Doughboy with a Flour Bag. The Doughboy is standing beside a bag of flour. Marked with a sticker: 1998 The Pillsbury Company. 3" in height, $5 to $8

Doughboy in front of Cabinet. The Doughboy is standing in front of a cabinet. Marked with a sticker: 1998 The Pillsbury Company. 3" in height, $5 to $8

Doughboy on Cupcake Magnet. The Doughboy has made a chair of his cupcake. Magnet is unmarked. The Pillsbury Company. 3" in height, $5 to $8

Poppin & Poppie Magnet. Poppin and Poppie magnets are made of a rubber like material. Magnets are unmarked. The Pillsbury Company. 2 1/2" Poppin & 2" Poppie, $12 to $15

Funfetti Hand Painted Magnet Set. These magnets were designed to go with the 1992 Funfetti set. The Doughboy is standing by a cupcake. Funfetti Magnets were sold two in a package. 1992 The Pillsbury Company, Benjamin & Medwin, Product Crafted in Taiwan. 2 1/2" in height, $16 to $25

Doughboy Mixing. With spoon and mixer the Doughboy prepares another one of his favorite treats. Marked with a sticker: 2000 The Pillsbury Company, Benjamin and Medwin NY, NY, Made in China. 3" in height, $5 to $8

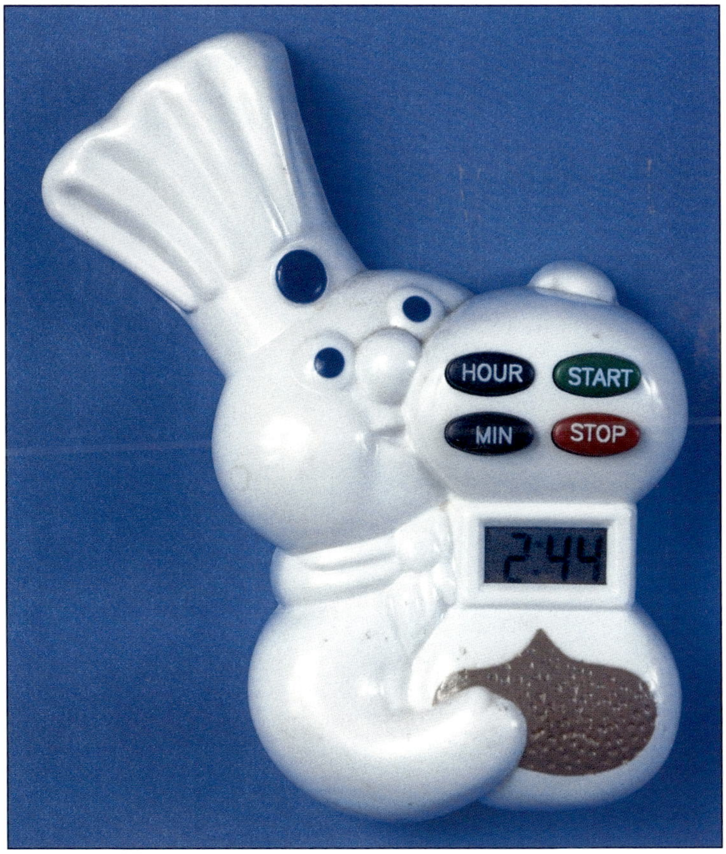

Doughboy Magnet Timer. The Doughboy will keep time with this digital timer that has hour, minute, start and stop buttons. Timer is marked on back: 1992 The Pillsbury Company, China. 4" in height, $10 to $15

Chapter 9

Christmas Items

Illustrated are items to decorate for Christmas. Find all kinds of Christmas ornaments, party lights, Doughboy porcelain Christmas tree, and so much more you just have to look.

Poppin' Up Fun, Heirloom Collection. The Doughboy is putting the finishing touches on his colorful house. Ornament is marked on the bottom. Distributed by: Carlton Cards, 1998 The Pillsbury Company. 3" in height, $22 to $30

50th Anniversary Bake Off Tin. This Bake Off tin comes with 3 ornaments inside. The ornaments are named Blue Ribbon, Wholesome Ingredients, and Blue Ribbon Recipes. Blue Ribbon recipe book is filled with actual recipes. All items are marked. Distributed by: Carlton Cards, 1999 The Pillsbury Company. Tin measures: 4 1/4" x 6 1/4", $25 to $35

Doughboy Cookie Cart, Heirloom Collection. The Doughboy is pushing a cart of cookies. Doughboy is marked on the back. Distributed by: Carlton Cards, 1999 The Pillsbury Company. 2 1/4" in height, $25 to $30

Giggle Doughboy Holding a Candy Cane, Heirloom Collection. The Doughboy is wearing a mitt and apron. The Doughboy will giggle when you push the star at the top of the tree on the apron. Distributed by: Carlton Cards, 2000 The Pillsbury Company. 4" in height, $25 to $35

Pillsbury Cookie Christmas, Heirloom Collection. The Doughboy is wearing a chef's hat, a polka-dotted blue apron and a festive mitt. The Doughboy is circled by a cookie wreath with an iridescent bow. Push the yellow star on the wreath to make the Doughboy giggle— "Hoo Hoo!". Ornament is unmarked. Distributed by: Carlton Cards, 2001 The Pillsbury Company. 4" in height, $25 to $35

Poppin' Fresh Christmas, Heirloom Collection. The Doughboy holds a cookie chain and Poppin giggles when you push the star on his apron. Poppin is marked on the back of his head. Distributed by: Carlton Cards, 2002 The Pillsbury Company. 4 1/4" in height, $25 to $30

Meringue-y Christmas!, Heirloom Collection. The Doughboy is shown placing a star on the top of a meringue Christmas tree. A recipe card was included for Mint Kissed Meringue cookies. When you push the blue ornament on his red apron the Doughboy will giggle. The date can be located under the red bow in the back. Distributed by: Carlton Cards, 2003 The Pillsbury Company. 4 1/2" in height, $25 to $30

Doughboy with String Puppet. The Doughboy appears to be dancing along with his gingerbread puppet. Doughboy is marked on the back of the head: 1995 The Pillsbury Company. 2 1/4" in height, $20 to $30

Pillsbury Doughboy Ornament Set. The Doughboy is featured on each of two resin ornaments. Standing on three frosted cookies wrapped with red ribbon and a bow. The Doughboy wears a cookie wreath saying Happy Holidays. The second ornament has the Doughboy with a towel draped over his arm holding a wire whisk, in the other hand he has a finished cake. Beside him is a rolling pin and canister of sugar. Ornaments are marked on the bottom: 2003 The Pillsbury Company. 3 3/4" in height, $15 to $25

Doughboy on Cupcake Glass Ornament. The Doughboy is sitting on top of a pastel colored cupcake. Ornament is not marked. Kringle Glass, Made in Colombia for Kurt S Adler Inc. 6" in height, $30 to $35

Rocking Doughboy. The Doughboy is riding a rocking horse. The ornament is unmarked. The Pillsbury Company. 3 3/4" in height, $6 to $10

Sitting on a Present. The Doughboy is sitting on top of a bright red package with a green ribbon and bow. The ornament is unmarked. The Pillsbury Company. 3 1/2" in height, $6 to $10

Doughboy Party Lights. Light strand is 12 feet long, with 12 lights, each light has a plastic Doughboy figure that fits over the light, and has an end to end plug to connect up other strings. Lights are safe to use indoor or outdoor. Box is marked: 1999 The Pillsbury Company. 4" Doughboys, $20 to $25

Peace of Cake. The Doughboy is holding a gingerbread cookie in his hands, while sitting on a rolling pin swinging from a cookie cutter. Across the cookie cutter is a red ribbon with the name of the ornament "Peace of Cake". Item is marked on the back of the red ribbon. 1997 The Pillsbury Company, Made in China, Matrix® LTD. 3 1/2" in height, $6 to $15

Christmas Pop-up Greeting Cards. Contents: 12 Christmas Cards with envelopes and 2 sets of recipe cards. The Doughboy pops up with a new recipe when you open the festive card. Made in 1997 by Creative Horizons for The Pillsbury Company. $20 to $25

Pillsbury Holiday Foil. This wonderful gift wrap foil paper features the Doughboy with an assortment of candies and cookies. 2003 Pillsbury Company, Jessica Stewart Collection. 24" x 10', $9 to $15

Doughboy Christmas Tree. This beautiful tree is lit by red, green, and yellow lights. It is decorated with 17 Doughboys figures, cookies, utensils, and Pillsbury medallion ornaments. A numbered Certificate of Authenticity comes with each tree. Tree is marked on the bottom of base: 2002 Danbury Mint. Mounted on the stand the tree is 15" in height. $120 to $140

Santa's Little Helper. Santa stands behind the table wearing a red suit and a white apron with red strips, trimmed in green, and the word Santa is written on the top of the apron. On top of the table the Doughboy stands on a cookbook. Scattered on the table top is a cookie Christmas tree, flour canister, rolling pin, cutting board, and a star cookie cutter. There is a bag of flour on the floor next to the table. Marked on the bottom of base: 2000 The Pillsbury Company, Danbury Mint, Crafted in China. 9 1/2" tall, $75 to $90

Happy Holiday Sweat Shirt. This navy blue, long sleeve sweat shirt shows the Doughboy wearing a green apron and red mitts, surrounded by an assortment of cookies. Happy Holidays is written below the Doughboy. The sweat shirt is marked: 2002 The Pillsbury Company. $25 to $35

The Pillsbury Doughboy Ornament Collection

This collection has 12 festive ornaments featuring the Doughboy. These ornaments are made of fine porcelain and hand painted. Each ornament is described below. Set comes with a numbered Certificate of Authenticity. 2000 The Pillsbury Company, Danbury Mint.

Gumdrop Goodies. The Doughboy holds a spoon with red and green sugar-sparkled gumdrops. 3 1/4" in height, $10 to $15

Building The Snowman. The Doughboy wears red mittens to decorate the snowman as he reaches to the snowman's hat. Sugar crystals make the snowman sparkle, black buttons, a green scarf and the black hat completes the snowman's costume. 3" in height, $10 to $15

Doughboy Surprise. This ornament makes it appear that the Doughboy just jumped out of a red present trimmed with green ribbon. 3 1/4" in height, $10 to $15

Kiss The Cook. To make sure he gets a kiss the Doughboy wears his favorite Kiss the Cook apron and holds a piece of mistletoe over his head. 3 3/4" in height, $10 to $15

Sledding Delight. The Doughboy rides on a sleigh that is made of candy canes for runners and a cookie for the seat. 3 1/2" in height, $10 to $15

Out On a Limb. The Doughboy stands inside a green tree. 3 3/4" in height, $10 to $15

Gingerbread Reindeer. The Doughboy sits astride a gingerbread reindeer. 3 1/2" in height, $10 to $15

Christmas Cupcake. Writing Noel with his yellow decorating bag the Doughboy finishes a red cupcake. 3" in height, $10 to $15

Holiday Roll. With his green and red stripped mitts the Doughboy holds a cinnamon roll. 3" in height, $10 to $15

Skating Enchant-Mint. The Doughboy skates across a red and white mint. 3 1/2" in height, $10 to $15

Christmas Stocking. The Doughboy places two candy canes inside a green and red stocking. 3" in height, $10 to $15

Making His List. With a red and green pencil the Doughboy makes his Christmas dinner menu. 3" in height, $10 to $15

Chapter 10

Children's Items

The Doughboy knows how to have fun and what better way then with his baking set. The Doughboy Poppin and Poppie wind up toys are always a hit when they go walking across the table. The semi truck and the all terrain vehicle sounds like the real thing. The Pillsbury Playhouse is designed for the finger puppets. The fun keeps going featuring a variety of toys and puzzles.

Doughboy Cookie Jar. The plastic cookie jar has been sold with or without the children's utensil set (shown in the next picture). Cookie jar is unmarked. 1996 The Pillsbury Company, China. 11" in height, $15 to $20 without contents, $30 to $40 with contents. Contents shown on the next page.

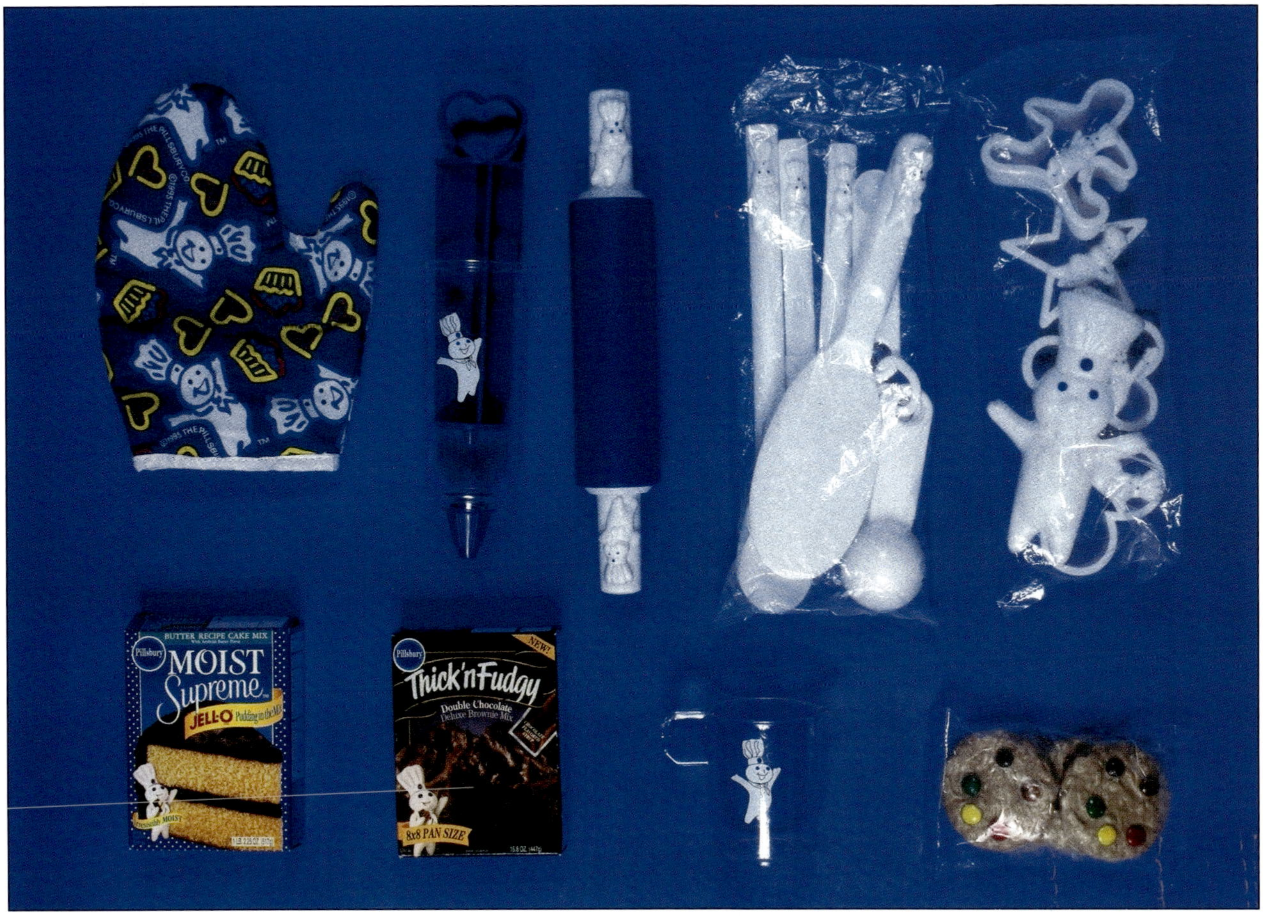

Nine items came inside the large plastic Doughboy cookie jar. These items were also sold as a separate set. Items and prices are listed separately below. Cake mixes are not priced. Set came with 2 cake mixes, marked, 1995 TPC, box size 3 3/4" x 2 3/4". Other items are described below.

1995 The Pillsbury Company Mitt. This blue mitt is decorated with the Doughboy, hearts, and cupcakes. By each Doughboy is printed: 1995 The Pillsbury Co. $2 to $5

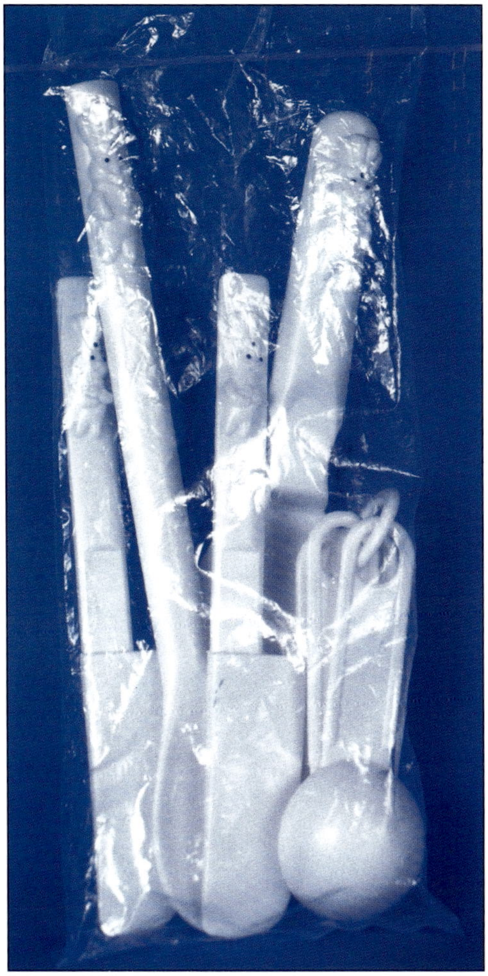

Utensil Set. Consist of 2 spatulas, a serving knife, measuring spoons, and a mixing spoon. Except for the measuring spoons, each item has a raised Doughboy on the handle. Utensils are unmarked. Set $5 to $10

Rolling Pin. Blue and white plastic rolling pin has a raised Doughboy on the handles. Rolling pin is unmarked. 8 1/4" in length, $4 to $8

Cake/Cookie Decorator. The decorator is made of plastic and has a blue insert. The decorator has a decal of the Doughboy applied to the front. Decorator is unmarked. 7", $3 to $7

1/2 Cup Measure. Plastic measuring cup will measure up to 1/2 cup. Marked: China. $2 to $4

4 Cookie Cutters & Doughboy. Set consists of 4 cookie cutters: star, gingerbread man, heart, flower, and a plastic Doughboy. Each cookie cutter has a small Doughboy on the top of the cutter. Cookie cutters are unmarked. $3 to $8

4 Plastic Cookies. These cookies looks like the real thing, decorated with red, green, brown, yellow, and tan candy like pieces. Cookies are unmarked. 2" in diameter, $1 to $3

Doughboy Sound Machine Semi. Honk if you Love The Doughboy Truck, made of metal. Sounds like a real semi-truck when you push the starter to activate the engine and lights. Push the horn button to sound the horn. Truck is marked on the driver door. 1999 The Pillsbury Company, made by Nylint Toy. 5 1/2" W x 20" L, $45 to $55

All Terrain Vchicle. Made of metal and hard plastic. Push the button to activate the motor starting, horn honking, and the engine running sounds. Vehicle is marked on the bottom. 2000 The Pillsbury Company, Nylint Toy. 11 1/2" long x 5 1/2" wide x 5" tall, $18 to $30

Melamine Doughboy. 3 piece Plastic Child's Set includes: Plate, Bowl, and Cup. This colorful child's set is decorated with the alphabet circling each piece and the Doughboy in the center. The set is marked on the bottom: 2000 TPC, Do not use in microwave, made in China. Plate is 9" in diameter, $14 to $20 for the set

Hot Wheels 1:24 Scale Nascar, #43 John Andretti. This car is in its original sealed box. The Doughboy appears on the rear fender. Box is marked: 2000 Mattel Inc. 8" L x 3" wide x 2 1/4" high, $20 to $28

Doughboy Soccer Ball. This colorful soccer ball depicts the Doughboy in each of the colored pentagons. Soccer ball is unmarked. 1998 The Pillsbury Company, made by Rawling. 8 1/2" in diameter, $28 to $38

Doughboy Grands Nascar, #43 Richard Petty car driven by John Andretti. This car was a promotional item from Grands Biscuits. The car is unmarked. 2002 The Pillsbury Company. 3" L x 1 1/8" wide x 3/4" high, $18 to $23

Hot Wheels Motor Coach, #43 John Andretti. This motor coach comes with a John Andretti trading card. The Doughboy appears on the side of the motor coach. Coach is marked on bottom: 2002 Mattel Inc. 5" L x 1 5/8" W x 2" H, $15 to $20

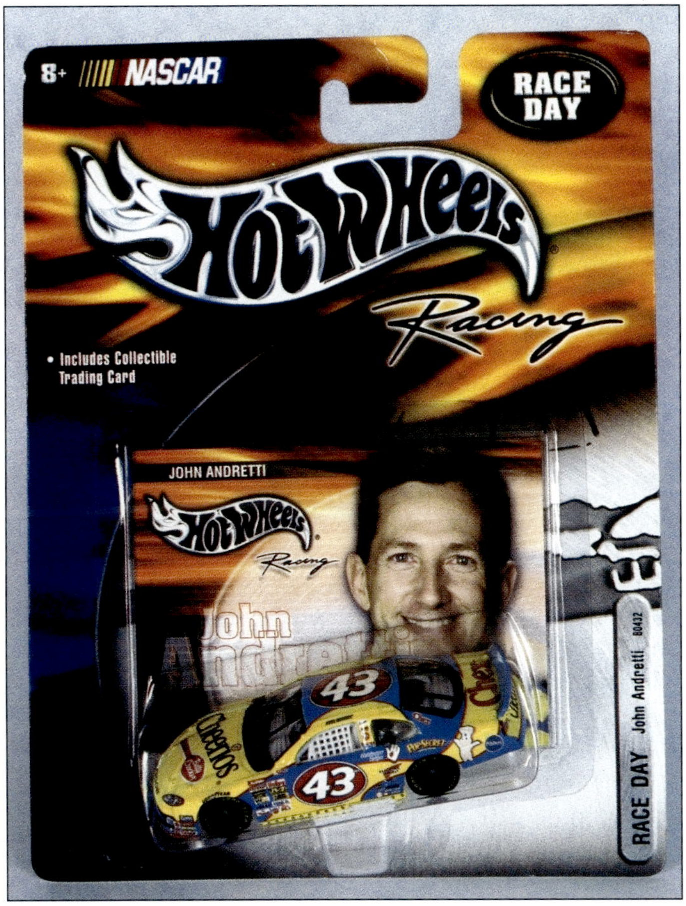

Hot Wheels Nascar 1:64 Scale, #43 John Andretti. This car is one of the small Hot Wheels cars. It comes with a John Andretti trading card. The Doughboy can be found on the rear fender. The car is in it original sealed package. Date can be found on package. 2000 Mattel Inc. $10 to $15

Doughboy Marbles. There are two marbles shown. Marbles are sold separately. Marbles are not marked, $5 to $8

Doughboy Puzzle in a Tin. The Doughboy's picture is on the front and back of the metal container and an 80 piece jig saw puzzle comes inside. Can is marked on the back: 2000 T. P. C. Tin is 9" in diameter, $15 to $20

Doughboy Back Pack Pal. This plush Doughboy back pack will hold many items, lift the kerchief in the back to reveal a zipper to insert your belongings. Back pack has blue straps for easy wearing. The back pack has a sewed in tag that is marked: 1998 The Pillsbury Company, Made in China. $20 to $30

Pez Dispenser. Pez dispenser is in its original package. No manufactured date is on the package. Pez Candy Inc. 5" in height, $30 to $33

Doughboy and Poppie Wind Up Toys. They actually walk when you wind them up. Wind up toys made in the 1970's. Toys are unmarked. Each is 3" in height, imported from China, $60 to $70 as a set

Pillsbury Playhouse. This house was designed for the Doughboy finger puppet family. There are four rooms in the house, each labeled with a name: Poppin, Poppie, Popper and Bun Bun. A latch on top of the house allows you to open the back for easy access. The house can be carried with the plastic strap at the top of the house. House is blue and white, the traditional colors of the Doughboy. Inside the house are shelves with chairs for the figures to sit on. On the back is a place for your name and address. It is hard to find these houses in mint condition, due to the played condition. Because the house was made of plastic and vinyl material, the shelves in the house tend to crack or break easily. 1974 The Pillsbury Company. 11" wide x 13 1/2" tall x 3" deep. House and four finger puppets $210 to $250. House, $90 to $130

Poppin Fresh Pop-Up Puppet. The Doughboy will pop into action when you insert your hand in the bottom of this puppet. Container is made of plastic, is opened on the bottom to insert your hand in the puppet, and comes with a plastic lid that features an impression of Poppin and Poppie. Marked: 1974 The Pillsbury Company, Pillsbury Playthings®. Can is 4 3/4" in height, Puppet extends 5 1/2" above container. $65 to $75

Poppie Fresh Pop-up Puppet. Poppie will pop into action when you insert your hand in the bottom of this puppet. Container is made of plastic, is opened on the bottom to insert your hand in the puppet, and comes with a plastic lid that features an impression of Poppin and Poppie. Marked: 1974 The Pillsbury Company, Pillsbury Playthings®. Can is 4 3/4" in height, Puppet extends 5 1/2" above container. $55 to $65

Chapter 11

Office Items

Write down all those special notes and dates with the Doughboy pen and pencil set. The note pad holder holds a pad of paper for easy note taking and the large calendar gives you lots of room to record those special occasions or appointments.

Doughboy Note Pad Holder. The Doughboy is designed to hold a pen or pencil in his right hand and the attached flour sack holds a note pad. Pencil is not included. Holder is marked on the bottom: 2000 The Pillsbury Company, Benjamin & Medwin NY, NY, Made in China. 5 1/2" in height, $20 to $25

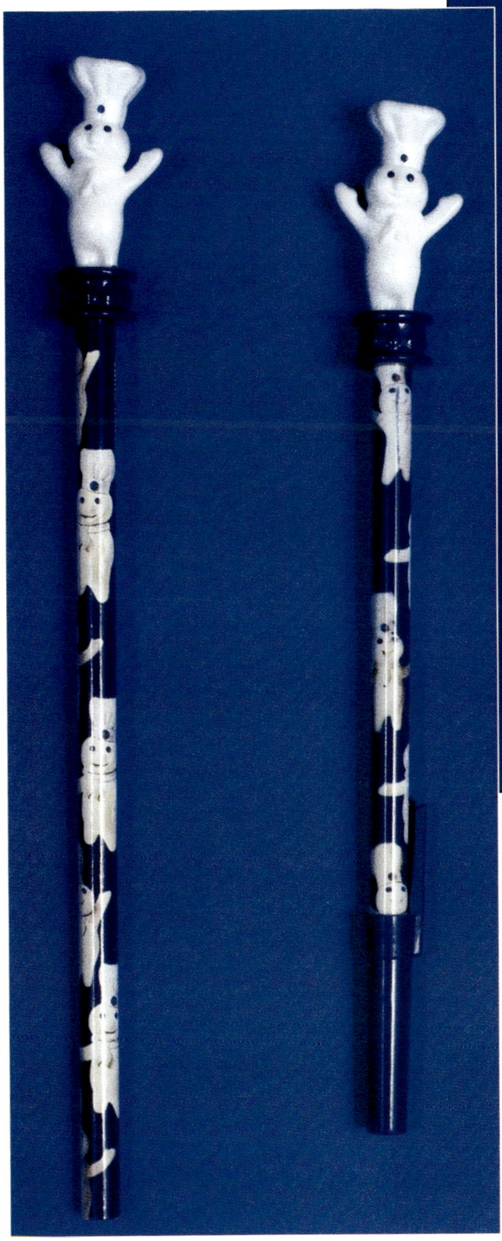

Doughboy Pen & Pencil Set. A small plastic Doughboy is attached to the top of each pen and pencil in the set. The shaft of each pen and pencil is decorated with Doughboys. Pen and Pencils are marked: 1999 The Pillsbury Company. The pen and pencil came as a set. $6 to $8

Doughboy Decorative Tacks. 12 Pack, Doughboy decorative tacks have three poses of four tacks each. Package is marked: 1998 The Pillsbury Company, Creative Imaginations Inc., Made in Taiwan. $13 to $18

2004 Jumbo Calendar. Blue and white checkered background accents this calendar, with a large picture of the Doughboy on the front. There is 12 different poses of the Doughboy one for each month. This calendar gives you plenty of room to write those important notes or appointments. A sticker sheet is included. Marked: 2003 The Pillsbury Company. Global Innovations, LLC. Calendar opens to 14" wide x 19" high, $12 to $16

Doughboy Bookmark. Featuring the Doughboy with General Mills "G". Made of a paper like material with a glossy finish and cloth tassel. These were given to employees when the companies merged. Bookmark is unmarked. 1 3/4" x 6 3/4", $5 to $8

Doughboy-General Mills Highlighter. Made of plastic with green, yellow, and pink highlighters at each point. These were given to employees when the companies merged in 2001. Highlighter is unmarked. 3 1/2", $5 to $8

Chapter 12

Pillsbury Bake-off Plate Collection

Three-Dimensional Collector Plates

Eight three-dimensional plates are in this series. Plates are all made of porcelain. Each plate captures the Doughboy making an award winning recipe and comes with the recipe card. Plates are numbered as a set. The first plate comes with a Certificate of Registration each additional plate comes with a Certificate of Ownership. Each plate is described below.

Kiss Me Cake. A three-dimensional collector plate displaying the warmth of the countryside. The Doughboy holds the winning cake that has been awarded the blue ribbon. The plate is made of porcelain, sculptured to capture the fine detail that makes this plate special. To enhance the detailing it was hand painted with vivid colors. Plate came with the 1999 winning recipe. The plate is marked on the back: 1999 The Pillsbury Company, Danbury Mint. 6 1/4" in diameter, $45 to $55

Peanut Blossom Cookies. A three dimensional collector plate presents the Doughboy holding a winning cookie as he sets on a counter top next to a vintage cash register. The plate is made of fine porcelain and sculptured to exhibit fine detailing that makes this plate charming. Cookie recipe was included with this plate. The plate is marked on the back: 2000 The Pillsbury Company, Danbury Mint. 6 1/4" in diameter, $45 to $55

Tunnel of Fudge Cake. This three dimensional plate is expertly sculptured to bring out the detailing of this hand painted plate. The Doughboy sits on a crescent roll, a spoon in his hands, paddling down the tunnel of fudge. The Doughboy has found another award winning recipe which is included with this plate. It is marked on the back: 2001 The Pillsbury Company, Danbury Mint. 6 1/4" in diameter, $45 to $55

Italian Zucchini Crescent Pie. This three dimensional plate captures the detailing of an old vintage kitchen with an opened faced oven and all the ingredients the Doughboy needs to make the award winning recipe. The plate is made of fine porcelain, professionally sculptured and hand painted to bring out all the detail. Recipe is included with the plate. Plate is marked on the back: 2001 The Pillsbury Company, Danbury Mint. 6 1/4" in diameter, $45 to $55

Poppin Fresh Barbecups. This three dimensional plate shows the Doughboy standing on a kitchen counter spooning batter into a pan for baking. From the enamel coffee pot to the recipe card box, all the detailing has been captured that could make this kitchen home. This plate is made of fine porcelain, hand painted to bring out the detail. The award winning recipe, "Barbecups", comes with this item. Plate is marked on the back: 2001 The Pillsbury Company, Danbury Mint. 6 1/4" in diameter, $45 to $55

Chocolate Praline Layer Cake. This three dimensional plate displays a southern setting. The Doughboy is dressed in a black jacket, ready to serve a slice of cake from a table covered with a pink polka-dot and flowered tablecloth. Recipe, "Chocolate Praline Layer Cake", was included with this plate. Made of fine porcelains, hand painted and sculptured to bring out all the detail. It is marked on the back: 2001 The Pillsbury Company, Danbury Mint. 6 1/4" in diameter, $45 to $55

Dilly Casserole Bread. This three dimensional plate has freshly baked bread sitting on a vintage stove. The Doughboy is holding a wooden spoon to mix the bread ingredients in a blue bowl. Hand painted to bring out the detailing, made of fine porcelain, this plate comes with the award winning recipe. It is marked on the back: 2001 The Pillsbury Company, Danbury Mint. 6 1/4" in diameter, $45 to $55

Magic Marshmallow Crescent Puffs. This three dimensional plate has an umbrella shading the table where the Doughboy sits holding a basket of crescent puffs. A coffee pot, the paper "The Pillsbury News", and a first place blue ribbon sits to one side of the Doughboy. A pink and lavender shopping bag sits on the other side of the table. Recipe is included with the plate, made of fine porcelain, and hand painted. Plate is marked on the back: 2001 The Pillsbury Company, Danbury Mint. 6 1/4" in diameter, $45 to $55

Chapter 13

Unusual Items and Miscellaneous

Find all those unusual and miscellaneous items in this area. Gumball machines, jewelry, watches, Doughboy slippers, and ties are some of the items you will find.

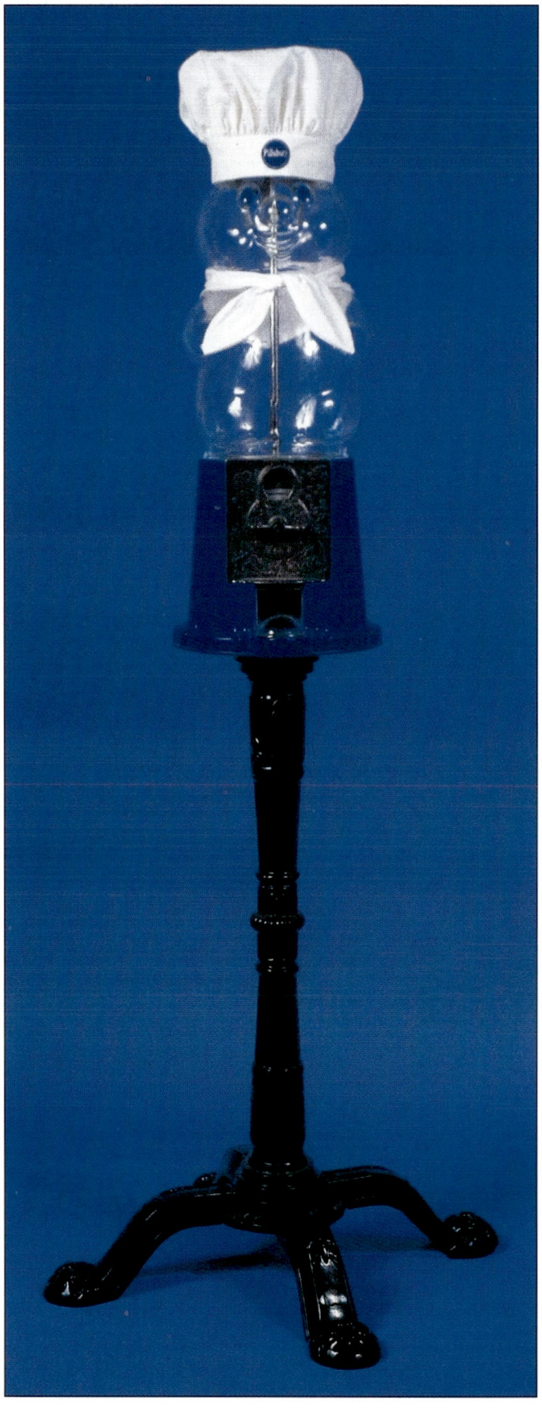

Pillsbury Doughboy 25th Birthday Gumball Dispenser with Stand. The gumball machine has a clear globe in the shape of the Doughboy. He wears his trademark chef's hat and scarf. The gumball machine was made for the Doughboy's 25th birthday. It has a plaque on the back of the machine that states, Carousel Pillsbury Doughboy 25th Birthday and a serial number which was issued to each machine.1990 by Carousel. 8" diameter at base of gumball machine; 21" in height, stand is 23" in height, $225 to $275 with stand, without stand $170 to $195

Doughboy Gumball Machine. A raised image of the Doughboy appears in three different areas on this clear globe. The Doughboy appears to be popping out of the globe. Gumball machine is marked with a sticker on the bottom. 2000 The Pillsbury Company. The gumball machine is 6" round at the base, 13" in height, $30 to $40

AM/FM Clip-on Radio with Earphones. This radio can be tuned to any AM/FM station. The radio has a clip on the back. Radio came with a headphone or earphones and needs 2 AAA batteries. The radio is marked on the back. 1985 The Pillsbury Company, Made in Hong Kong, 7" in height, $40 to $55

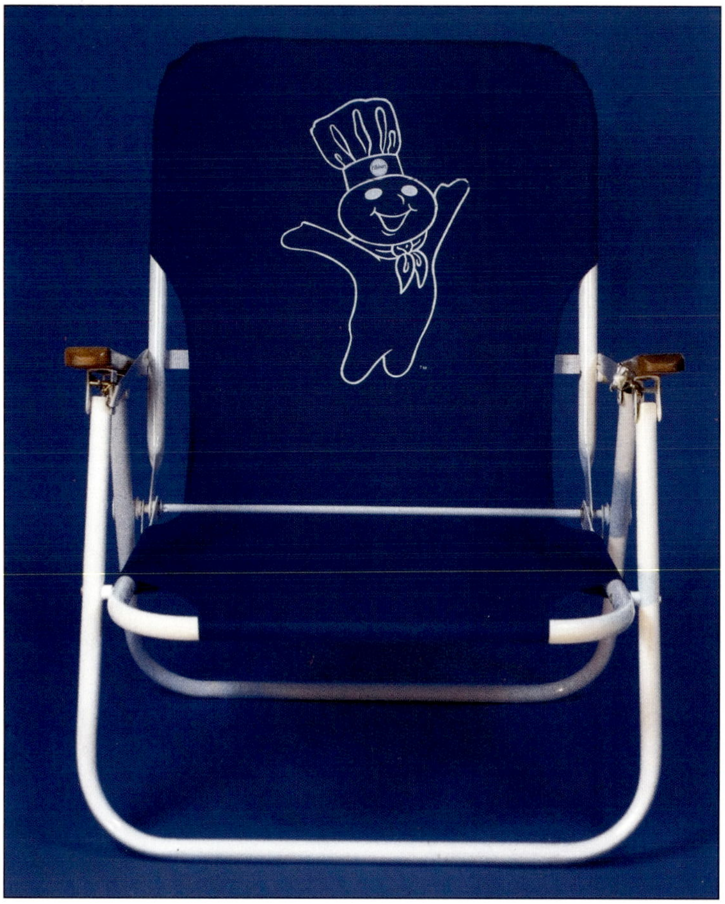

Beach Set 3 pieces. The chair has the Doughboy on the seatback, made of a blue nylon like material, with a pouch attached to the back of the chair for storage of lotion and other items with a Velcro closure at the top. The terry towel has an embroider Doughboy in one corner of both ends of the towel. Made of 100% cotton in the USA by Danbee. Towel is 34"W x 67"L. The umbrella is blue and white ribbed. On each white panel the Doughboy appears. The umbrella can be used as a beach umbrella or you can attach the wooden handle for carrying. Umbrella opens to 48" in diameter. Information obtained on these items is that they were a premium offer to Pillsbury representatives in 1997. The items have no other markings or labels indicating that they are Pillsbury items. $140 to $160 for 3 piece set

Pop Up Recipe Greeting Cards. The greeting card set contains 12 cards with envelopes and 2 of each of the recipe cards, one to send with the card and one to keep for your baking enjoyment. There is an assortment of birthday cards, thinking of you, and get well soon. Box is marked. 1996 The Pillsbury Company, Made by Creative Horizons LLC. $18 to $25

Can Cooler Sleeve. Made for the General Mills and Pillsbury merger, it reads "Together Even Better". Front and back pictures shown. Made of Neoprene material. Can cooler is unmarked. $5 to $8

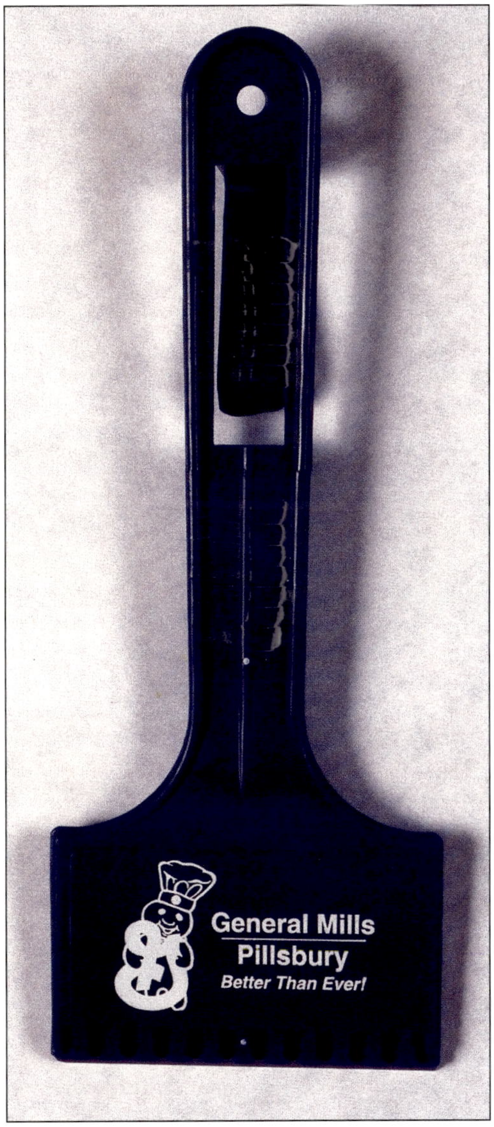

Window Scraper. Made of plastic, it features the Doughboy holding a "G" for General Mills. The item was made for the merger of General Mills and Pillsbury Company. Scraper is unmarked. 9" in length, $7 to $10

Doughboy Earrings. The earrings are all white except for the Doughboy's blue eyes. Earrings come on a card marked: 1996 The Pillsbury Company, The Walter Heimter Company NY. 1" in height, $20 to $25

Pillsbury Doughboy Hatpin. A die-cast two-tone pin in cooper and brass colors, it also makes a great lapel pin. Pin is marked on the back, T. P. C. Made in the USA. $12 to $18

Doughboy Ring. The ring band is silver in color. The Doughboy is white with blue eyes and a little red heart on his body. The ring is adjustable. Maker and year of manufacture can only be found on the attached card when originally sold. 1996 The Pillsbury Company, The Walter Heimter Company NY, Made in USA. $18 to $23

Doughboy Watch & Tin. This watch has two Doughboys and 5 mixing bowls scattered about the face of the watch. The Doughboy goes around the watch band in a repeated pattern. Watch is marked on the back. 1997, Nelsonic. Tin measures 3 3/4" in diameter, $55 to $65

Doughboy Wrist Watch. The watch features the Doughboy on the face. This item could only be ordered with proof of purchase seal. Marked on the dial: 1987 The Pillsbury Company, $12 to $18

Badge. This badge was worn by a Pillsbury representative to promote their frozen dinner rolls and biscuits. The badge has a picture of the Doughboy holding a dinner roll on one side and a biscuit on the other. No other markings are on the badge. $10 to $20

Doughboy 2000 Countdown Watch. The watch has the Doughboy on the face of the dial and a blue leather band. The watch features, day/clock or day/dual time, year, month, day, alarm, stopwatch and two countdowns. Watch comes in a tin container. Marked on the back of tin: 1999 The Pillsbury Company, Made in China. Metal tin measures; 8 1/2" long x 2 3/4" wide, $15 to $20

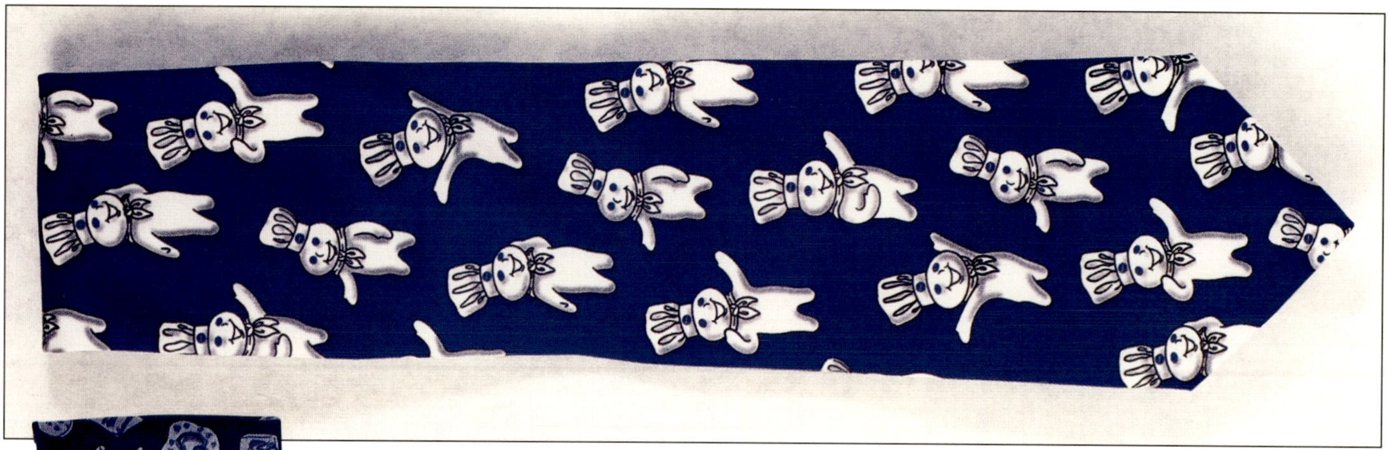

Pillsbury Doughboy Repeat Tie. This blue tie displays the Doughboy in several different poses in a repeated pattern. The tie is marked on the inside: 1996 The Pillsbury Company, Ralph Marlin. $20 to $25

Pillsbury Doughboy Picnic Tie. This tie is red and black checked with picnic baskets featuring the Doughboy. The tie is marked on the inside: 1999 The Pillsbury Company, Ralph Marlin. $20 to $25

Pillsbury Doughboy Cookie Tie. One Doughboy is featured on this tie with utensils, rolling pins, and baked goodies in the background. The tie is marked on the inside: 1998 The Pillsbury Company, Ralph Marlin. $20 to $25

Doughboy Key Chain. The Doughboy has a 1-1/2" metal ring attached to the top of the chef's hat to hold keys. Key chain is marked on the back: 1998 The Pillsbury Company, Made in China. Doughboy is 3" in height, $15 to $18

Doughboy "G" Key Chain. The key chain is made of a rubber material with a shiny finish and a metal ring. Key chain is unmarked. 3 3/4" in length including ring, $5 to $8

Pillsbury Doughboy T-Shirt. These T-shirts came in different colors and sizes. The T-shirt is printed with the saying, "Nothing says lovin' like something from the oven!" Date is shown on the shirt under the Doughboy. 2002 The Pillsbury Company. $15 to $20

Pillsbury Doughboy T-Shirt. A dark blue T-shirt features a 15" Doughboy. Gildan Activewear, 2000 The Pillsbury Company. $22 to $30

Doughboy Men's Sleep Pant. Sleep pants are 100% cotton, featuring the Doughboy. The pants have side pockets, roomy fit, and a drawstring waistband for added comfort. 2003 The Pillsbury Company, $13 to $25

Doughboy Slippers. The slippers feature the Doughboy with his hands reaching upward, wearing his chef's hat and scarf. The slippers are soft, have cushioned sides for warmth, and made of all man made materials. Marked on the label inside: 1999 The Pillsbury Company, S G Footwear Co., Made in China. $35 to $45

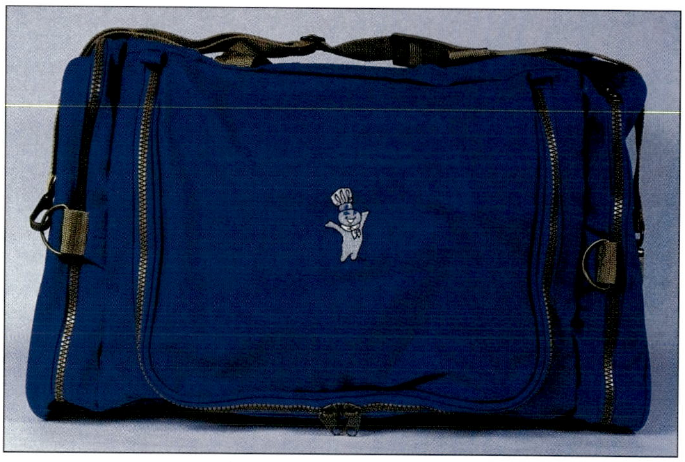

Doughboy Duffle Bag. Bag has a large compartment with a zipper, 4 smaller zippered pockets on the outside, and one side pouch to slip items in easily. Duffle bag comes with two handles for carrying and a removable shoulder strap. Embroidered on the top of the bag is a 2 3/4" Doughboy. Duffle bag is unmarked. 24" W x 14" D x 14" H, $30 to $40

References

Information in this book was gathered from many internet sources. The web pages consulted are listed below.

http://www.pillsbury.com
http://www.generalmills.com
http://www.generalmills.com/corporate/about/history/hist_flash.asp
http://www.generalmills.com/corporate/about/history/hist_doughboy.pdf
http://www.generalmills.com/corporate/about/history/hist_bakeoff.pdf

Index